Bipolar Co

By Harriet Dyer

This book is dedicated to my most wonderful mum, Skylar, dad, Joe and my lovely friends xx

Changed some names so I don't get sued. If you're offended by something you think is about you - Don't worry, it's definitely not :)

Bipolar Comedian

1.) Hello

My name is Harriet Dyer. I was born in Kingston upon Thames, London on the 15th November 1983 which I always feel a fraud saying because "being from Cornwall" is a lot of my shtick onstage. I should probably mention who I am here because it's most likely you haven't heard of me. I'm a stand-up comedian and this is a book about my life.

"But why would we care if we haven't heard of you?"

Even though I'm only 36 I've had quite the colourful life, I've struggled the whole time with mental illness and have only really accepted that in later years but since doing so have found there's far less of a sense of impending doom, in fact I think I'd go as far as to say I'm happy - Which has been a long time coming. I would've liked to have read something like this when I was growing up so I wouldn't have felt so alone and the feelings I felt weren't wrong, I needed a little bit of help.

If anyone can find any comfort in what I've been through that'd be great. Also for selfish reasons, it's nice to evacuate the brain guff from time to time, so think of this book as a vacation for my head too.

I don't have any memories of London really. My first memory is on an exercise bike at my aunty Mavis's house. The bike came with the house, she never even used it. Aunty Mavis was a stern "Mrs Trunchball" type character who oddly enough was a viral sensation in 2010 for teaching a cat to sing Nessun Dorma.

My mum and dad were very trendy, they looked like models. I don't think of them back then to be in colour if that makes sense as the only photo's I've seen of them are in black and white. My dad looked like Joe Wilkinson and my mum looked like Twiggy.

Mum was such a gentle soul, there was a child-like innocence to her. She never smoked or drank, was so kind hearted and honest, would never put herself in front of anyone and was fucking hilarious but in a way where you had to get to know her first to get the full Vivian Dyer experience.

Dad was handsome, very charming, apparently all the ladies fancied him. They both had such lovely London friends, two being married couple Nora and Dave who sadly must be long dead by now as they were elderly all those years ago. Even though I only met them very young I remember them radiating such warmth and kindness.

We stayed at theirs once and Nora put me to bed with a massive soft toy and regularly checked on me throughout the night to make sure it hadn't suffocated me to death.

Another time Nora, Dave and mum and dad were all in their conservatory, (someone did well) I was outside in the

garden and Nora said, "It's nice Harriet brought a ball to play with" seeing me with a red round object to which my mum replied, "She didn't" and it was at that moment I took said 'ball,' kicked it in the air and it exploded in my own face. The 'ball' was one of Dave's prize winning tomatoes.

We moved to Cornwall when I was four. I became who I am in Cornwall. We moved because my dad was stressed and run down. Stress manifests itself in the strangest of ways: his elbow enflamed and became massive, he wore a Tubigrip to try and squash it down. I have a clearer idea now as to why he was so stressed but at the time it was just put down to pressures of London life because the moment we settled in Cornwall the elbow did deflate. My dad was a civil servant and to be honest I'm still not sure what that is so we'll say it's something to do with ice-cream and lizards. So yes, I can see why a job in such a field would have been so stressful.

The house we moved in to in Cornwall had no furniture in it, I'm not sure why no-one had thought to source any in advance. There were dust sheets everywhere and we had a black and white TV and we were sitting on the floor, watching it and eating chips, I'd never been so happy.

The house was overlooking a river, it's the house that to this day my family still live in. We put it up for sale once but I don't think anyone wanted it so we stayed. My dad was originally from Cornwall, brought up on a farm in the 1950s. I never met his dad, my grandpa but from what I've been told he was quite the character. Dads mother was a lot more serious, she lived until she was 93 and was in the land army, although her best mate Margaret (still alive at 99) says she was a lazy bugger and let her do all the work.

My mum was from Yorkshire, she left home at 15 as she felt she didn't belong. Looking back now I think she suffered with depression, I think they both did. Worry would always eat her up, it was always worrying for others too, never herself. That was literally her only fault, that she cared too much.

Despite this I was a daddy's girl growing up, I definitely wasn't as close with my mum then and I've no idea why, to be honest it breaks my heart a bit as it was time wasted without the bond we had in later life.

Dad took me everywhere. We never had a car so everything was a mission, we'd walk for three miles every Sunday to do the main food shop and dad would let me get a drink for on the way back. I'd choose a tomato juice which was a questionable choice for someone so young.

Dad took me to the ballet once which still to this day remains one of the best days of my life, it was amazing. Goodness knows what it was called or what happened but I remember watching smiling away with those little red binoculars and at the end they all got blown away by the wind (spoiler) and as a result were darting around the stage with umbrellas. I'd never seen anything like it, we got back so late as got the coach back, I remember falling asleep in dads arms feeling so safe and special.

He also used to take us to a scrap yard on a Sunday where we'd gather junk to make robots with. We held hands wherever we went, I didn't think it to be strange because it's what we'd always done but we were still doing it years later when I started secondary school and a kid that lived down the road said we should stop because it was weird to which I said, "Thank you for your concern Ben Shelby but I heard you ate a dog shit sandwich at a party so I shall not be trusting your judgement on this occasion" because that's how I spoke.

Grown-ups can be strange in what they feel threatened by and for some reason people that lived nearby took a dislike to us when we first moved to the area without even meeting us. The only thing I can think of is that they thought we thought we were better than them. There was a women that used to get the younger lads to shout, "Skinny bitch" at my mum from the bus when they'd see her doing the school run.

I'm pushed to think of many people I grew up with that went on to "do something" with their lives. No-one seems to ever leaves Cornwall or they save up their whole life to take a holiday, to Devon.

We took a holiday to Devon once, my mum was pregnant with my little brother. We discussed names for him, I suggested, 'Heady' if he was born without a head but she didn't seem keen.

We went to watch Dick Whittington the pantomime where they asked the audience if any kids would like to come up on to the stage. They didn't pick me but I ran onstage anyway. I took the mic from the leading lady and wouldn't stop waffling on, wasn't fussed at all that there were hundreds of people just staring at me like, "Is this part of the show?"

I was asked what I had in my hand, to which I replied, "This is my Sylvanian Family otter, Joseph. He's called that because my mum's got a baby in her tummy and that's what she's going to call him, not 'Heady' as she hopes he will have a head."

All the kids were given goody bags and were told to leave the stage but there weren't enough for me, apparently my bottom lip started wobbling and then as if it was all planned, the good fairy came down from the rafters with a goody bag. It was quite the magical experience.

Then like out of a Hollywood film as I was making my way back from the stage a guy a row in front of my parents apparently turned to them and said, "I've been in theatre for years and let me tell you this, there's something special about her, she's got stage presence" and then he took a puff of his cigar and twiddled his moustache (of course that bit wasn't true but the rest was). Mum and dad were chuffed with that and I'm not sure if that was the start of it but they always seemed to know that I wouldn't end up with a "normal job" and definitely understood and accepted that which I'm very grateful for because a lot of parents don't.

For a long time my ambition was "to be a boy." Mum caught me in the bath when I was five crying, "I thought I would've grown a willy by now."

In primary school I went to the toilet, a bully followed me, burst through the door behind me snarling,

"I've heard you want to be a boy, is this true?"
"Yes, sure is"
"Oh" and with that she put the door back on its hinges and off she went.

I was encouraged to be different, be silly and make full use of the wonderful imagination I'd acquired from reading so many books. Books were everything from when I was old enough to know what to do with one, I was more like a book boa constrictor than worm.

Dad plonked me in the bath when I was constipated once with a wonderfully illustrated book on dinosaurs and all sorts of other splendid things and I remember making up little games with myself for each page, I had such a fun time. Although I'm still not sure why I was just left in a bath for constipation and for a full day. Ah well, pruning is a small prize to pay for such a percolated imagination.

Mum came to pick me up from primary school once and I was waiting there with 25 other kids, my mum was like, "Um… Hi? What are you all doing here?" to which they all chorussed, "Harriet's having a party!" I'd told everyone I was having a party and no-one's mum bothered to check with mine, they just left them there,

"Oh bloody 'eck Harriet" said mum and she didn't have a car so had to walk all 25 children the two miles home like The Pied Piper of little Cornish idiots.

When finally home she didn't have any party food so gave each child a little bit of a roast dinner on a ghostbusters paper plate but gravy on paper plate was such a rookie mistake and all sloppy hell broke loose.

Having said this I'm not sure if planned the party would've been much different as mum avoided giving me processed foods which backfired as I once went to a party, ate a whole bowl of Smarties, downed a bottle of coke then was so giddy on e numbers that I punched the birthday girl in the face using a My Little Pony as a Knuckle Duster.

Another time I turned up to school with an eye patch on, all the mums gathered around asking my mum, "Goodness, what happened to Harriet's eye?" to which my mum replied, "Oh nothing, she's wearing it for attention."

ADHD wasn't a thing when I was at school but if it was I definitely would've been diagnosed with it. I couldn't concentrate or seem to tune in to the way of learning that school had to offer. I could feel myself falling by the way side as all the other kids started to academically do better than me, the only thing I seemed to excel in was making up daft stories. Here are some, word for word that I found in some old school notebooks when I cleared out the attic of the house I grew up in a few years ago. Spoiler alert: I have a baby brother by now - Joseph (or Joe as he's known).

The Sea Monster

It all started when mummy, daddy, Joe and I were in a big ship and suddenly we saw a long head in the distance. We went over to where we saw the monster but when we got there it was gone so mummy, daddy, Joe and I put a wetsuit, oxygen mask and goggles on each. We all dived in the water when suddenly I saw the sea monster. It had a scabies neck, two horns and it smelt. But suddenly it saw us, swished its tail and chased after us. Luckily I had a penknife with me so I stabbed it but it got me and I sank slowly into the water. A pint of blood came out of me and mummy, daddy and Joe started crying but I swam up and swung the monster around by its neck, I felt like Superman. I never saw the monster again. Someone said they saw him at the airport wearing sunglasses about to take a far away trip.

A Big Black Spider

One day I was in a really big jungle, suddenly I looked up and saw a big black spider and it said to me, "Please may you get rain to us because our crops are drying up" so I said, "OK." So I contacted Mr Frost and the other weather people and said, "Make it happen. Please."

It rained and rained for days and days. For four weeks until it stopped and the spider said, "How can I repay you?" I said, "Can I see where you live?" and he said, "Yes" so he showed me where his house was and I put some gold bars in my pockets to take home but a guard spider saw me and arrested me.

Suddenly I woke up and found out that I was dreaming with a pillow over my head. My mum came in and I told her all about it, then I sneezed and reached into my dressing gown for a tissue… You'll never guess what I found?! I found the gold bars! Was it true or wasn't it true? I gave the gold bars to my mum because she said she needed a new kitchen.

Invisible

I came round the corner and saw a strange shaped bottle in the gutter. Inside there some purple liquid which seemed to be frothing and bubbling. I took the bottle home and then foolishly tasted the purple liquid. Immediately I felt very strange and when I looked in the mirror there was nothing there.

I decided to have some fun, so went out to see if I could play some tricks on babies. It was working out my day because a baby's pram came over the hill. I lifted up the baby's hat and to the baby and everyone else it looked like it was floating in the air. Soon I got fed up with that so I went to the airport. I got in an aeroplane and sat in the drivers place. I pressed the start button and up in the air I went. But somehow the real driver had got on the plane and the purple liquid was starting to wear off. I pressed off on the plane and started to run, but the driver caught me and after some explaining the driver let me go. I went home and looked in the mirror and had a big shock as I had not turned back into me. I was a little dog.

Looking through these stories now in the books I'm not sure my teacher appreciated my creative flair as his response to them all was to put in red pen underneath, "Interesting Harriet."

2.) Love thy neighbour

I had a neighbour, "Gordon" we'll call him because I don't want to get sued. He's actual name is one of the other tank engines. I think he was about four years older than me and I really looked up to him, pretty sure I was an absolute joke to him though. We spent a lot of time together because he was always left alone as his mum had left and his dad was useless and off with a new lady.

When you're younger you never want to admit that you haven't tried something, especially to someone you look up to so when he had cigarettes and asked if I'd ever tried smoking I lied and said I had. I think he knew I hadn't and told me to take a drag and breath in as hard as I could so did and was coughing and spluttering so hard and he was in hysterics. He asked me if I wanted to try some Kiwi 20/20 to which I had no idea what it was (it's cheap fruity booze from back in the day) but said yes (I don't know why I didn't learn, it was always a trap) he kept spitting in it and for some reason I still drank it because he told me to.

Because he was always so mean the bar for what was considered nice became so low. Sometimes he'd hide behind a wall when I'd leave home and he'd jump out and smash me in the face with a basketball and I'd think, "Ooh, someone's keen today!"

Where we lived a block of flats and ten houses all shared a yard at the back that kids of the residents all used to play in, many came and went. There was one kid that lived four doors down from us, he had a toddler sister that seemed possessed, no matter what time of year she'd sprint out of her house in just a nappy, just screaming and running until somebody caught her. Once she left the yard and almost made it as far as Tesco, her nappy disintegrating as she ran.

Once when round their house the banshee toddlers brother asked if I wanted to see something cool.

"Yes, always"
"Right, get in this wardrobe!"

With that we watched his older sister and her boyfriend have sex through a gap in the wardrobe. I was only nine, I wasn't sure what I was watching but whatever it was, it didn't sit right.

With Gordon being older than me he was curious sexually and a lot more developed than I was. I thought he was the best thing ever but looking back he had ginger curtains so I can't imagine he was desirable to many others than me. I was desperate to please him and an easy target.

When I was ten he'd want us to write down "What we wanted to do to each other" on little pieces of paper, fold them up, put them in a bowl then draw them out and do them to each other. I misunderstood the game entirely and put, "Make each other nice sandwiches for lunch" He took this as he should put his dick in my mouth.

No-one wants a dick sandwich Gordon!

It was all very destructive as he'd mock me for the fact my boobs weren't developed, he said he'd never seen a bra so small (I didn't even need a bra, mum just got it for me as she felt I'd been wearing Jurassic Park vests for too long, although even now I don't think there is too long for that.) He didn't take all this in to account and would still try to get me to give him a tit-wank (goodness knows where he'd even heard of that at that age) they were very confusing times.

People say that school's the best days of your life, to me this is absolute horse shite. I hated school so much and seemed to spend all my time preferring to be dead which sounds dramatic but was true. I found the confinements of it really difficult and even though I guess "I fitted in" with the popular lot (even though ugly they let me hang around because I was funny) I felt I didn't belong with anyone.

My mind always felt like a black cloud looming and if I ever opened up about how I really felt people would quickly become uncomfortable and wouldn't know what to do so I felt it best to keep everything suppressed.

My view of sex was obviously askew. By now I was ten at Primary school and was overly sexual, trying to play "mummies and daddies" to gather a gander of everyones bits.

I got called into the headmasters office twice, once because I'd apparently been far too aggressive playing kiss chase. The headmasters words were,

"Edward says you were showering him in violent kisses and he was very scared."
"It's not my fault Edward's a pussy."

Mum and dad seemingly had this marvellous relationship and I wanted nothing more than that. I'd ask boys out at school every day, I truly believed I was in love with them, they only had to speak to me and I'd think we were meant to be together.

The second jaunt to the headmasters office was because there were two people in my class that really liked each other but weren't doing anything about it so I wrote a letter to the girl pretending to be the boy saying, "Will you please hurry up and bend me over this table with your big hard dick." This was frowned upon.

One would've thought this would've been quite the red flag for a kid to come up with?

There was a badass kid that lived down the road from me, Ray, I really did love him, kind of still do in a way but a different love, a love where I really just want him to be ok as he was not well from such a young age.

One of the reasons I thought he was such a badass was because he once brought a squid to school (a dead one) he put it on the floor of the girls toilets, a teacher walked into the same toilets, slipped on it and cracked her head open on the sink.

He was in the year above me at school and I remember having to wash up my art stuff in the communal area and for some reason he was standing next to me. I wanted to impress him so much and knowing he was a badass I thought swearing would do it so was suddenly shouting, "Fucking hell, I can't believe how painty my fucking paintbrush is, what a fucking ballsack" he looked at me as if to say, "What an unnecessarily aggressive girl" and walked off.

3.) Jets and Sharks (well, the Cornish equivalent)

It was like an angel sent from heaven was drafted in for the last year of primary school - Thea. She was gentle and loyal with a beautiful soul. For some reason she liked me too and we became inseparable. Her family were great too, her mum reminded me of my mum and her dad had a proper twinkle in his eye, he was an artist and such a good one, their house was always chaotic but I liked that: it also had a really distinct smell to it that I now know to be weed. I'd stay over lots and they'd take me to cool places. I wasn't used to travelling by car, my stomach didn't have the disposition for it and I'd get travel sick. Once I was sick after we all went to McDonalds, they said their car never smelt the same again.

I remember them winning ten pounds on the lottery so kept taking treating us to trips and dinner on it saying, "You can thank the lottery win for this" they must have spent it fifty times over.

They were stylish too - Thea was the first person I saw wearing a pair of Vans, I remember being doubled over laughing because her mum had packed her 2 left shoes from completely different pairs for PE, she put them on and sort of waddled around giggling.

We'd camp in her garden, go to the corner shop for sweets, learn the raps to songs with rude words in and generally just be innocent, silly little girls.

That year flew by, secondary school was looming, although with Thea by my side it didn't need to, we were to be in the same class and whatever happened I knew I always had her.

We fitted in well, I instantly got on with a kid called Bill, we clicked. He was an interesting soul but the first person I met where I thought, "Oh, money can't buy you happiness after all."

I never went without anything but my school uniform when I started secondary school was from a charity shop etc so I think it's totally normal to romanticise how much better things would be if there was more money: it's easy to put that on a pedestal as the answer to everything, even now.

Bill was always allowed parties which we all thought was great but everything else wasn't so much. His dad had died when he was really young and his mum seemed a loose cannon: she clearly had mental health issues, was always erratic and was never home, I'm pretty sure she had a girlfriend and was always off with her. I was jealous then of his freedom but now feel for him as it was clearly a lonely existence.

We ended up going out with each other but he was a dick. There was a kid in our class with Cerebral Palsy, I assumed because had an ancillary with him it must've been harder for him to make friends. I got on with him and his ancillary well so started hanging out with them but Bill became jealous and on Valentine's Day in front of everyone he serenaded me with, "Roses are red, violets are blue, sorry but I'm dumping you!" I stood there baffled and humiliated whilst he spat, "Why don't you go out with the cripple instead?" Lovely.

Oddly I still tried to be Bill's friend after that, I think because he so adamantly blamed me which I didn't think to question, just assumed he must be right because he was clever and certain in how he felt.

A year or so into secondary school a girl called Tash transferred to our class for trying to stab someone in the one she was previously in. I got on really well with her, she was always nice to me, her friends were absolute cock weasels though - Them and the girls in my class had beef which stemmed from a party where Thea and another girl smooched. The cock weasels would shout that they were "Lezzers" and such nonsense which pissed us off. Tensions between the two parties would build up during each week then come to a head during PE. There was a girl in the other group we called Umpah Lumpa because she looked as though her favourite past-time was basting then marinating in a vat of fake tan which was actually quite pioneering because I'm sure fake tan didn't even exist back then?

We were playing Dodgeball one day, the atmosphere was tense and hostile. Umpah and a girl with a lisp were being so confrontational to my mate Belinda then Umpah threw a basketball in her face. Belinda and Umpah started a full on fist fight and all my girls were just standing there staring. "Fuck this" I thought so ran over and got the girl with a lisp in a headlock but Tash was not having this and ran over, grabbed me and literally launched me across the room like a javelin!

Previous to this I was civil with the opposing girls as we had science lessons together but they were absolutely livid with me that day. I didn't understand what I'd done wrong because I was sure it was two on one their end but they seemed to think I'd made it the other way around: perhaps they mistook Umpah for a basketball?

4.) Confusement

Mum felt it would be confusing to explain sex to me because I always had boys as friends. I very much wished she had because living with what happened with Gordon was more confusing as I had no idea how the science behind it all worked and would now spend every hour of every day genuinely thinking I was pregnant. It was so stressful, my school work was suffering and the experience as a whole became an ordeal because every thought paled in insignificance to this overwhelming worry that I was going to have to have a baby and my parents would be so upset with me. One lunchtime I cracked and confessed my woes to a girl in my class and she snapped, "You can't be pregnant because you haven't even started your periods yet!" I was so relieved that I didn't even think about what a shit friend she was.

I definitely put my dad on a pedestal (until writing this I genuinely thought it was "pedalstool" and when the incorrect spelling read line kept appearing I thought, "well this spellchecker must be broken"). I saw my dad as one of those dads you get in films that's perfect; that makes robots, helps with school projects, well, the stuff that dads should do with their kids really.

In actuality dad was facing some inner turmoil and one day he didn't come home which was so unlike him, so much so that us and all our neighbours were out looking for him.

Dad was gay and born in the late 1940s on a farm in Cornwall. Cornwall can be backwards at the best of times, let alone then. I can only imagine how awful it was for him as not only could he not be himself but as being gay was illegal then it was installed into society that it was not only wrong but against the law too. No wonder people's feelings were "closeted," they were forced in there.

What he shouldn't have done however was drag my lovely mother through it all.

Him not coming home on that day released a torrent of slop which then became his routine, he'd just disappear with various men for days and when he'd finally come back he'd expect to slot back in to family life, slipping back in the marital bed like nothing ever happened. It was a constant head fuck because mum and I would be upset (Joe was too young to know what was going on) but dad would act easy breezy, like all this chaos was completely normal which made us question ourselves - Were we overreacting in thinking he was being unreasonable in wanting to be out playing the field with men but expecting to come home to family life with us after?

Dad was now spending money meant for our family on his new life, mum was cast aside. She became the soul looker afterer of my brother and I.

He started to dress differently too (I'd never seen so much leather) and his taste in music went from Motown to a never ending trance montage. I asked him for a stick of chewing gum once, he said to go in his bag and there I found a massive tub of lube. Another time I was on my way to the toilet, looked in his and mums' bedroom as knew he was in there and there he was on the computer ogling a guy that was naked apart from a pair of Dr Martens and a massive boner. In my head that guy was German but upon reflection, how would I know that from a picture? I asked dad what he was doing and he panicked and said, "I'm just shopping for new boots."

Once we were in Pizza Hut all sat around a table and my dad was pulling strange faces, I followed his gaze and learnt he was giving the eye to this man who was also eating dinner with his family. Dad must've had a platinum gaydar because the guy appeared to be doing funny looks back and then they both disappeared to the toilets for a while. No wonder Pizza Hut went to shit and they named it Pasta Hut for about a week after.

I think this sort of thing went on far more than I realised because now I look back on it, when I was really young he'd often be off on "work trips" so no doubt he was up to all sorts then, but I was just blinded by the postcard and toy he'd bring back.

He needed to leave, a dad and husband to a lady shouldn't be behaving like this, he needed to pick which life he wanted and that was exactly it, he didn't want to. When I'd tell him this he'd get nasty, on a couple of occasions he threw the TV remote control at my head, it obviously struck a nerve, as well as my head. I started to hate him because I felt he'd broken our lovely family but now of course I know that wasn't true, he just felt a way which meant everything as a result would be different and would hurt people he loved which led him to act out.

We had a fish and chip dinner one night, mum and dad had a massive argument in the middle of it, fish and chips were thrown everywhere in rage and afterwards Joe and I went round sadly picking it all up off the floor, eating it then getting in to the bath and crying. And it's quality family moments like that you just can't put a price on.

Joe and I were so different, to the point where it was sometimes baffling we came from the same concoction but it was little moments like that we bonded over. My favourite thing we'd do was a game we made up called, "The Pasty People." I'd get in bed with him, usually on a Sunday as it's a well known fact God loves a pasty - We'd pretend the duvet was pastry, one of us would be either steak, swede, onion or potato and the other would be 'the gristle' and the object of the game was to escape the perils of the gristle. Still my favourite game to date and with Joe being four to five years younger then me (depending on time of year) I got away with playing it far later than I probably should have.

We all trundled off on a, "Let's fix the marriage family holiday" because nothing says let's fix the marriage more than bringing the kids along. It was an absolute debacle because spoiler alert: You can't "fix" gay!

Dad obviously had lovers back home and whenever we'd go to a tourist attraction he'd be in the gift shop sourcing souvenirs for them.

We stayed in a family room and I have a vivid memory of a light snapping on at about one in the morning to see dad trying to sneak out of the door and mum barking, "Where are you going?" He hadn't banked on getting caught so hadn't had time to come up with a lie so simply whimpered, "I'm off to the red light district." "If you leave now, you'll never see us again" and with that he reverse tiptoed back into bed and nothing was said of it again.

Dad's actions made mum so ill. It's painful to see photos of her around that time because she was a shell of a human, all the stress had caused her to lose any weight she had on her. I don't think dad ever understood the enormity of how it affected her, she'd never been with anyone else other than him, he was all she knew and loved.

Having said that dads stress elbow came back, he tried to squash it down with a thousand jumpers but still if ever any kid from school saw my dad out and about they'd always come back to me with,

"Harriet what's with your dads massive elbow?"

The more dad wouldn't leave the more I would play outside. I was 12 now but still only allowed to stay within the perimeter of the yard. I loved to cycle though, it used to clear my head (no child should need to clear their head) and when I say, "Yard" it was just a patch of concrete where the cars would park. Joe would cycle around and around in the same circle, get bored and meanderingly throw himself on to the floor. Mum would be watching from the kitchen window and would shout, "Oh bloody heck, he's flopped himself off again".

Off I went on my bicycle with no regard to the yard. An older kid (we'll call him MC) started to pay me attention, I thought he was very cool as he looked like he wouldn't look out of place in the boyband East 17 and he could do that thing on a bicycle where you go along doing a wheelie seemingly for ever.

He knew I had a penchant for a 'Boglin' (90s toy craze, Google if unsure) he told me he had the limited edition glow in the dark range and asked if I fancied seeing it so off I followed him with the promise of those. He led me in to his garage, I couldn't see any Boglin's anywhere, he grabbed me, pushed me over, tied me up and for hours he continually raped me.

He decided that wasn't enough and this was now what I would be to him whenever he wanted, at his disposal. He said if I told anyone he'd kill my little brother but I'm not sure it had the desired effect when I replied, "But he's already been killed six times this week by the gristle."

I considered myself to be an outsider before but now I was so outside I had to get out a periscope in order to even gander a glimmer at what the outside could be.

I'd stay in to avoid, well everything but then I'd get threatening letters about what he'd do to my family so it was easier to just let him do what he wanted. I became so withdrawn.

5.) Existing

My so called friends problems became tedious. "Having a meltdown because they hadn't been bought a new horse for a birthday" kind of tedious. Most of the people in my class were at least middle class, I don't know whether it was down to that, that our lives were too different or down to what I was going through was too much for anyone so young to comprehend - Perhaps a bit of all the above.

I regrettably confided in a smug couple in my class because MC had given me a letter than said that he was going to slit my throat which made me somewhat concerned. The couple decided that because in the letter 'meet' as in "I will meet you" was spelt 'meat' as in "I will meet you with a sausage" I must have written it myself. They circulated this throughout the class and as a result everyone thought I was a liar, I was crushed.

I started to hang around with a different group of people, ones I felt understood me more (were just more troubled I guess). At every school there's always a kid who's mum has a party round hers whilst she's there and gets all the kids booze. At the time thoughts are, "What a legend, she's so lucky having a mum like that" but looking back, it's actually really fucking concerning.

I'm 13 by now and this woman's getting me two three litre bottles of White Lightning and I got absolutely hammered. No-one spoke to me when I arrived, it was mainly older boys there and they did that thing where they clocked me but because I wasn't considered 'fit' / couldn't benefit them in any way they pretended they hadn't. I stood there awkwardly but because of everything that had happened I realised I knew how to pique the interest of such idiots so shouted, "Does anyone want me to suck their dick?" These twins piped up, locked me in a bathroom and I "sucked their dicks" although in truth I just blew on them a little bit because I didn't really know what I was doing, just took instruction from the title, "Blow job" like I had a row of bottles in front of me.

I then rewarded myself by collapsing in the living room and projectile vomiting into an empty box of Heineken. No-one checked if I was ok, they just looked and rolled their eyes with disgust: I couldn't be there a minute longer so suddenly bolted upright and ran out the door with the intention of going home but woke up the next morning underneath a lamppost surrounded my swans. Those swans looked after me far better than anyone at the party did.

I had a friend who got her kid taken away from her because she left her with a group of swans but if you can't leave your kids with something that's protected by the queen who can you leave them with? I said it in court and I'd say it again. The same persons mum used to jump out of a bush at me on my walk to school, she'd have a bottle of vodka in her hand and a wonky wig on her head. I realise this paragraph contains a lot of information.

After 'blow job twin gate' and my horrific hangover the next day I was so muddled so thought that perhaps the encounter could mean something. I saw the bigger picture, that forming a partnership with a boy with very swift access to another boy could keep me safer.

Optimistically I wrote a letter to one of the twins asking him to be my boyfriend because nothing says long term relationship like blowing on your twin brothers dick.

He read it out on the bus in front of everyone and they all laughed at how stupid I was thinking something could possibly come from that. Then because my surname's Dyer, for the rest of school days I would now be known as "Dyson." I BLEW!

All this combined with dad seemingly behaving like a completely different person led me to have my first breakdown at 13. I had a little cardboard lid with damp cotton wool in it with rocks lay on top (I must have gotten confused with cress) and I'd only speak to them. I remember once being invited to a party, turned up but wouldn't speak to anyone other than my rocks and stood there mapping out "the constellations the rocks were originally from" in the condensation on the person whose party it was' window.

Mum was worried so took me to the doctor who said I had M.E but looking back I think I was just broken, confused and withdrawn. He wanted to put me on Prozac but what parent would want their kid on Prozac at 13? Mum declined the offer saying, "She doesn't need that, she's just eccentric."

One perk occurred in the coming years - Due to "the M.E" I got to pretty much pick and choose when / if I went to school which was fantastic and when it came to exams I just rocked up to do said exams then rocked off after, pardon the pun.

In my head Gordon and I had some kind of relationship so when he got girlfriends or even just spent time with girls he actually liked I'd feel devastated. He was with one girl for a while and she was beautiful, curvy, everything I wasn't. She had a friend that was very rogue and for someone so young he was very switched on about the world, simply didn't give a fuck and I liked that. They were hanging out after school, Gordon asked if I'd like to join them, I WAS SO EXCITED as like I said I never really belonged anywhere so when I'd get little nuggets of opportunity with people I really liked I'd think, "Oh perhaps this is where I could fit in" even if it meant spending time with someone Gordon held in far higher regard than me.

I waited in the rain for two hours for them but they never showed up. I went home crying and mum dried me off and gave me the biggest cuddle.

6.) Quite the soirée

Gordon had a party, it was like something out of the film, 'Kids.' I invited Thea and everybody fell in love with her. Gordon made me eat cat food in front of everyone and then I snogged a guy that no-one else would kiss and when he kissed me it was like his jaw disconnected like a Black mamba which was awful. I'd never known anyone to be turned on by the sweet, sweet taste of IAMS.

He devoured me in one but luckily I had my phone on me so rang Thea from the pit of his carcass to come and rescue me.

Thea and I decided we'd rather go to Tesco to get sweets and head back to mine to watch Comic Relief.

Around this time a murder had occurred, I'm not even sure if it had happened in Cornwall but what I vividly recollect was that police were looking for a white van that was at the scene.

On the way to Tesco there were no street lights by a large carpark in front of a garage with shutters rattling in the wind and in front of the rattling and darkness was a solitary white van with its lights on just there in what we found a most menacing fashion. Of course we assumed it was the van of murder so sprinted off and once out of breath jumped into a nearby bush for safety. We stayed there huffing and puffing and after a while I thought, "I'm sure it's not only mine and Thea's huffing and puffing I can hear" so turned around and sure enough there was a guy behind me in a cagoule [always a cagoule] vigorously wanking.

I exited the bush at full speed dragging Thea by her hood, what an eventful evening.

7.) Creative outlet

In the same way my silly stories used to make me happy, my newest form of escapism was drama and acting; I absolutely loved it.

My parents suggested Cornwall Youth Theatre which became another place I didn't fit in, but still attended for years because it was one of the few places in Cornwall I could act.

Once day we were all sitting in a large group talking about the shows we were doing and I was sitting next to a really beautiful girl, let's call her Analyse; (because I think that was her name) I remember having a really itchy hand so was scratching it. After a while she suddenly jumped up and shouted, "What on earth are you doing?" I looked down and realised I was scratching her hand thinking it was mine. Everyone thought I was strange and Analyse didn't come back after that.

A splinter group was formed and I met this girl called Saffie I became obsessed with. I don't know what it was, in fact I do know what it was, she was selfish and I could never do enough for her so I always wanted to one day do enough.

I used to get obsessed with people, like I wouldn't be able to sleep as I'd be wide awake, lay there, thinking about them. It made me question my sexuality because it was mainly girls I felt this way about. Now I realise I just loved people but not in *that* way: animal, vegetable or mineral, I would just love, invest and overthink.

Saffie and I went to different schools. I once walked three miles to meet her from her school in the rainiest rain I ever did see, I was completely drenched, like just walked into the sea drenched. We then walked into town (which was another couple of miles) she'd never have any money but was always hungry and wanting this and that so I'd pay for it all because I always had a job (first a paper round where I was paid £5.21 for 521 papers which I got sacked from because I hid them in the river and then a green grocers where I was paid to wipe the mould off the fruit then put back on shelves). Saffie would try to rob make-up in Superdrug so I'd end up buying it for her too to avoid us getting arrested.

She'd invite me to parties and gatherings where everyone would be so happy to see her but take one look at me and, "Why on earth have you brought this weirdo" would flicker in their eyes.

There was a patch of grass known as, 'The Green Blob' where we'd drink and hangout when there was nowhere else to go. I'd trot on down the hill to the Tesco (this Tesco features quite heavily in this book) to try and get served as I was a year older than everyone else and had a grown woman's face even though was still only 16 myself. One time a girl from schools' sister was on the till, I was filling up the conveyor belt with booze…

Her: *Looking at me suspiciously* "I think you were in my underage sisters year at school"
Me: "Nah, I don't even know Gemma"

It's dangerous the amount of pressure put on kids to do well in their GCSE's, I wouldn't even open my results in front of everyone. I got on a bus and went to the beach to sit on a cliff like an absolute emo, (not an emu like my mum says) I needed four C's or above to go to college and that's exactly what I got, I was over the moon and couldn't believe I'd done it. It was all I wanted but now I didn't have anyone to tell, I tried to strike up a conversation with the seagulls flying by about it but they didn't seem interested.

8.) So long school, you fucker!

When I started college all I wanted to do was drama but the only drama course was 60% theory and to be honest, very dull. I did media studies too and that was better, there were some people from primary school I'd previously known so that was good as we'd always gotten on and there were a lot more chances to be creative and to be left to our own devices within that course.

College life seemed a lot less stifling, there was a lot more freedom. There were smoking areas, a pub nearby, lots of new and interesting people from all over; people that didn't know anything about me. I definitely was treating it as more of a social liberation rather than actually getting an education. I wanted to have a laugh and get fucked up, that's what was making me happy. If I wasn't at college I was at the pub, often spending "lunch time" at the pub too, drinking and self medicating, what a terribly lovely pastime.

There was a teacher at college that projected she was this real caring hippy type: such a caring and gentle being but I've come across many people like her and that's all it is with them, a projection.

I came in one day with two black eyes courtesy of MC and in front of everyone the hippy's said, "What happened to you Harriet?" I said something dismissive / trying to be funny like, "I just wouldn't let things go so had to teach myself a lesson" which would get a forced chuckle.

Then I was sitting there after and thought, "Fuck it" so blurted out, "Actually, I didn't do it myself, it's this guy that lives by me, he's been abusing me for years now and I don't know what to do."

She paused for about three-seconds, then just carried on with the lesson and it wasn't mentioned again.

A few years ago I asked what happened to her because people like her are some of the worst and it bothered me to think of her doing the same with other people.

You'll never guess what happened to her? She had a massive dog which knocked her over whilst she was preparing dinner one evening, she ended up face planting a raw carrot and losing an eye!

It would appear I'm quite the authority in the vegetable community.

I wasn't lucky enough to be getting away with just black eyes, MC was still raping me. It was easier to let him rather than risk him carrying out the threats to my family he promised. One night he dragged me down by the river, was raping me with a knife to my throat and something clicked, I was done with "just going through with it" this was no way to live.

I slithered out from him like an eel, grabbed his arm, twisted it around, then his hand, then I snatched the knife and jabbed him with it as hard as I could in his side. I felt like Jackie Chan.

He slumped on me like a fat ox, repulsing me more than ever so I shoved him off which in doing so sort of rolled him into the river. I hoped that if the jab hadn't killed him he'd drown.

I'd like to say here, there is a part of me that feels bad wishing someone dead like that, I can safely say I haven't made a habit of it or indeed ever felt that way about anyone else: in that moment there and then that's what I felt driven to.

He didn't even drown. He just rested on top of all the papers I'd thrown in previously.

In all seriousness, I didn't know then that he didn't drown, I'd pushed him in then ran away so on top of everything else I now thought I was a murderer, it really was quite the burden.

College wasn't as fun any more. I confided in a girl I'd been in 'Greece The Musical' with as she let me believe I could talk to her about anything as we got on so well. She responded in the very helpful way of never speaking to me again.

It was the friend I'd met doing 'Westside Story' that helped the most. We're still dear friends now.

I'd actually known of Kelly since primary school, her mum used to help out at play times at school. Kelly's dad was 6ft 9 and was actually approached to be Darth Vader in the Star Wars films but he turned it down because he was in the navy at the time. Kelly and I had some great times, we really would have such a laugh and shared a lot of common interests like acting, pubs, lager and cigarettes.

We became very close and she mentioned that her local Amateur Dramatic Society were auditioning for The Wizard of Oz so we went along. She got the part of Dorothy and I got the part of Scarecrow which could not have gone better. Kelly lived between college and where rehearsals were so we'd go to hers after lessons in-between. We'd always have the exact same tea of super noodles with a slice of buttered white bread washed down with orange squash and then we'd head to rehearsals.

Sometimes we'd go to the pub and get pissed before rehearsals and that was even more fun. There was a good bunch of folk at Am Dram, they made us feel welcome. My knees were bruised black by the end of it all due to all the floppy legged falling down that Scarecrow does.

There's a scene in the stage version that's different to the film where Dorothy and Scarecrow go through this dark forest and I can't remember why but there's a bolder involved. I was supposed to throw it at Dorothy but I'd always lob it into the audience for a laugh instead but would pretend it was an accident. Kelly knew I did it on purpose even though I'd always deny it.

The learning of lines is what I found impossible, no matter what show I was in I'd cry to my poor mum, "Why have you let me do this?" as could never comprehend how all the lines would ever end up finding their way in my head, it was overwhelming. Mum had read somewhere that if you record what you need to learn on to a dictaphone and play it just before you go to bed at night all the information is supposed to saunter on in your head. She didn't have the money for a dictaphone at the time though so suggested I borrowed one from a lady called Peggy that lived down the road.

Peggy was the most Cornish woman I ever did meet, she'd always greet you with an, "All right there me bird!" She let me borrow her dictaphone, I got it home, pressed play on what was already on the tape and it was her tuned into the frequency of the police radios giving an audio commentary as they went and because it's Cornwall she of course knew everyone. "John's been nicking again he has, you don't a nickname like 'Sticky fingers' from having a penchant for preserve".

Whether it was psychosomatic or not, recording lines really helped.

One day I was late to Wizard of Oz rehearsals so I text Kelly saying,

"Got tattoo, running late, on way now"
"Oh Harriet, I bet it's like that awful one Mel C's got isn't it?"

I found this to be most insulting. There were two well known female tattoos in the public at that time and those were the barbed wire one that Mel C from Spice Girls had and the barbed wire one that Pamela Anderson had, both minging they were - Although to be honest now I'm not sure what I did get was much better; I got a squiggly man on my stomach with a very long finger.

I'm surprised I didn't get a full body of tattoo's done then as I've always had such an addictive personality.

In one week I'd gotten both my eyebrows, my lip, my nose and all down my ears pierced. Funnily enough my mum only let me get my ear lobes done on my sixteenth birthday and then the flood of piercings did cometh.

I bumped into my very Cornish grandma Betty in town just after I'd had all my piercings done and she squawked, "Bleddy eck 'Arriet, *(always a silent H down there)* you look like a Christmas tree!"

I got on well with the tattooist, he was tattooed literally everywhere other than his eyeballs and quite possibly the inside of his anus. I think he took a shining to me because for a short time I was in there very regularly and apparently I once did shots with him at a bar we frequented. He was the idiot that told me that when you do a tequila slammer - Instead of biting on a of slice lemon you're to take a bite out of a beer mat. I was doing this for years, no wonder everyone thought I was feral.

9.) A very lovely time

Through acting Kelly and I met an absolute legend called Holly and it really was a case of, 'How the other half live' as her house and all she owned really was stunning; going to hers was like stepping in to a completely different world. She was obviously from money but in no way stuck up or naive to actual issues. She loved an adventure too and was so kind.

Every Thursday a big group of us would go and do the pub quiz at The Globe pub. The Globe was brilliant, it was a really old pub and we didn't even need phones back then because no matter what time you went, you'd be sure to know at least some of the drinkers there. It was practically my home for years.

There was a girl in our pub quiz group that I most definitely would not invite, she was a friend of someone else but coincidentally happened to also be the 'girl with a lisp's' sister that I'd gotten in a headlock in that fight at school. She wasn't happy that I was now hanging out with them and decided to pour a whole pint on my head in the middle of the pub. It was a very cowardly thing to do as she did it when I was sitting down, had my back to her and then she walked off so didn't give me a chance to talk it through / kick off. I was so drunk I just sat there thinking the roof was leaking for ages.

The most frustrating part was I was staying at Holly's that night so stank like a hoppy ball-bag. The following week however, I was the only person to know a question about The Beastie Boys in the quiz which impressed her, she gave me a nod and we were cool from then on.

Holly's house was like a retreat. It was a massive old farm house on the outside but on the inside it was really modern. It was such a hub too, she'd always be hosting things like murder mystery nights and BBQ's that weren't all about plopping lumps of meat on fire - Everything was so well seasoned and marinated with so much to choose from AND we'd be drinking homemade sangria and playing croquet too.

It was fun, inviting, safe and homely to be there, it was quite the life. At her murder mystery night I was the murderer which I was well chuffed about because this time it was make believe. I was a German baddie with an eye patch, although if being honest I think I may have once again just given myself the eye patch. Everyone made such an effort and it was integral that we stayed in character from the moment we stepped through the door which really added to the atmosphere of it all. As I'm writing this I've got a big smile on my face as these really were such happy times.

Holly's brother was a little surfer dude, he must've been about seven when we went to Fistral Beach, Newquay to check out a surf competition and wangle freebies from the stalls. Said freebies included lots of Extreme Sports stickers. I'm not sure why but he asked me to stick a sticker on his leg which was massive, it practically covered the whole of it.

We had a lovely afternoon, parted ways and then that night Holly rang me from the hospital where she now was with her brother as apparently it was an industrial strength sticker and wasn't coming off his poor little leg so the hospital had to chop his leg off. Only joking but it was still quite the ordeal, a hospital trip that could've been avoided, I felt awful. What a way to reward such kindness, I can confidently say I haven't stuck a sticker on a child since.

10.) The waiting game

I was all over the shop when it came to men, didn't know what I thought, I wanted to be looked after but was obviously conflicted with all I'd been through. No-one ever fancied me (which was actually a good thing as it minimised options) so on the rare occasion that someone did, they'd become "my type."

A guy called Marco claimed to like me but I found him to be so complimentary that it seemed disingenuous so when he asked me out I said, "Could I possibly get to know you better first?" It turned out I was right, he was trying his luck with everyone in the hope someone would succumb to his advances because the moment I said that he moved on to the next.

His brother then started to show an interest. He seemed all right but was a bit flash for my liking, he was all about material things. Their parents owned a clotted cream factory and they always had money, nice cars and a speedboat but I couldn't give a shit. I ended up in some kind of relationship with him though through him not moving on to the next after badgering me. Perseverance prevailed I guess? He pushed for sex but I just didn't fancy him. We'd dry hump when I was stoned and pissed but I just couldn't bring myself to do anything else.

He'd comment on "how hairy my arms are" when he was so hairy, like couldn't see skin through all the hair hairy and skinny too, not that either of that matters but just the hypocrisy from someone that had the physique of a pipe cleaner.

I've always had style but just never a girly style, the style of a Cornish skateboarder I'd say but in pubs I'd wear a little t-shirt or a shirt on a "proper night out." Pipe Cleaner obviously didn't share the love for my style as he'd buy me dresses to wear.

It baffles me when people must be attracted to the person initially to have got with them but when they're with them they try to change them.

I'll never know why people feel the need to knock each other down in relationships instead of being, "Now I've got an ally, we can build each other up so it's us against the world, together."

The only time the Pipe Cleaner was anything other than a cocky little shite was after months of pestering me, I finally agreed to go on his speedboat. It wasn't for me, so queasy I did feel. He kept asking if I would like to drive it, "Really, have you met me? I'm an uncoordinated disaster!" Again, he kept on at me so I took the wheel and very nearly almost ploughed us in to a cliff. I definitely heard the Pipe Cleaner let out a whimper and for the rest of the afternoon a hostile silence filled the air.

11.) Time to recuperate

Dad had finally left the family home for good. The remaining family participants were broken so decided on a holiday to London to stay with auntie Mavis. FYI London is never a holiday destination, nowhere where there's that many people in a hurry can ever be classed as relaxing.

I started to develop flu type symptoms, I felt awful, wanted to stay in bed but Mavis was as sympathetic as a rabid goat so responded with, "Ok, we'll start you off gently with a trip on the London eye." The only thing worse than feeling awful is feeling awful whilst moving in a circular motion.

It was August so the underground was especially stifling, I felt I could collapse at any moment but was continuously told I was fine. I bought a souvenir mug for the Pipe Cleaner but swung it around in its bag, it hit a lamppost and it smashed into pieces which was the perfect metaphor for whatever it was we had going on.

We finally escaped auntie Mavis's clutches and got the train home. I put a Hula-Hoop (crisp) on each finger, went to the toilet and came back still with a Hula-Hoop on each finger, mum was livid because it was unhygienic and she was correct.

When back in Cornwall I wanted nothing more than to go home and hibernate but the Pipe Cleaner insisted on me coming out. We went to the pub, I drank through the pain. He didn't seem that chuffed with his gift, how very ungrateful.

The Piper Cleaner never drank as he always drove but he'd always ply everyone else with booze. I bumped in to an old pal who was training to be a hairdresser so in my delirious ill state agreed to have my hair cut in the pub toilets. With my new haircut the Pipe Cleaner wanted to go clubbing in Newquay. A pain engulfed my stomach but I felt it was nothing sambuca couldn't get me through and besides that I was hesitant to declare medical emergency as the previous week I'd been tarnished with a time wasting brush after I woke up after a night out, had rings on me and thought it was ringworm when it was actually marks where I'd been sticking flaming sambuca's to my stomach.

Unbeknown to me my appendix had burst and was quickly becoming gangrenous and what was I trying to do? Dance it off.

The club closed, I was really looking forward to going home as I desperately needed to lie down but of course the Pipe Cleaner wanted to go for a walk along the fucking beach. I hobbled along, we got back in his car, was this it, finally my chance to go home? No, I had these shorts on (of course I did, it's

Cornwall) which had a hole up the back of them (where I'd been skewered on some railings trying to accost a man that didn't treat a pal of mine very nicely) and the Pipe Cleaner was trying to put his creepy fingers through there. I asking him why his finger nails were so long and he said, "So I can run them up and down your silky skin"

"Sweet Jesus, I need to go home, immediately."

He finally took me home, by now the pain was ridiculous - I couldn't even make it to my own room, I had to get in my brothers bed (he wasn't there). Mums 'spidey senses' must've been tingling as she came in and the moment she saw me she called Kernow Doc out (Kernow is Cornish for Cornwall) and he said I was fine and with that he left. Luckily mum didn't believe him so called out the other doctor, (he used to be a vet and was a bit too pokey for my liking) his response was more, "Oh gosh, she's dying, get her to hospital immediately!"

An ambulance came, the paramedics took my blood and told me to hold cotton wool where the prick had been but my hands were spasming and I couldn't do anything other than maintain a locked gnarled claw stance which must have been due to the shock of it all.

Once at hospital a doctor kept asking me when I'd lost my virginity, I didn't then and still don't understand the relevance of that question. I was then rushed into surgery.

I died on the operating table and was brought back to life. Something people seem to ask upon hearing that is something along the lines of, "Did you see a light?" I didn't but I do remember seeing the tops of the surgeons heads which makes no sense because that means I'd have to be above them looking down, watching them work. A friend said, "Perhaps there were mirrors on the ceiling?" Where exactly is this hospital, Peter Stringfellow's bedroom?

12.) Death becomes me

As I was only 17 at the time I was in the children's ward. I made quite the arrival as got wheeled through after surgery at about 3am, I'd been fitted with a catheter, was off my tits on morphine and apparently woke all the kids up screaming, "Get this tube out of my fanny!"

The nurses were brilliant, such good people with such good chat. I immediately bonded with one nurse over Australian teenage soap, 'Heartbreak High' which was on at the same time every morning. There was a character in it called Drazic that I proper fancied; he was very rogue and a keen rollerblader which was a winning combo for me. All the nurses called me 'Pink Harriet' because I "had pink hair." I actually had red hair but didn't have the heart to correct them.

Kids on the ward tended to be, "Lifers" or in and out like a whippet; like brought in with a suspected appendicitis but turned out to be trapped wind, that kind of thing.

There was dog bite boy, he got mauled by a dog, snake bite boy who was getting it on with a girl on the beach, took his jacket off, a snake crawled in to it, then when he went to put it back on said snake bit his hand and it swelled up so much it looked like when you blow up a rubber glove.

When I said, "Lifers" I meant the one's that were in for a really long time but of course, sadly some didn't get to leave hospital to have a life.

I couldn't believe the amount of people that came to visit me in hospital. The Pipe Cleaner was the first to come, "What's this?" he asked before squeezing my catheter. I'm not sure why he didn't wait for an answer, what did he think it was, a Capri Sun? He didn't visit again and bizarrely told a lot of people the nurses said I was to have no visitors to try and stop people coming to see me. I wasn't sure why we weren't done before but that definitely cemented the end.

I found it overwhelming when people visited as they'd all be gathered around my bed, talking across me to each other very loudly which felt like everything was closing in. Everyone always had the same look on their face when they'd first see me too, a look of surprise because I looked like… well, like I'd just died.

Thea came to visit once with a plant for me, she'd put water in it but nothing underneath to catch it so it was pouring everywhere. She was confused by what was happening and kept spinning around trying to find someone to help with the situation she'd found herself in.

After a couple of weeks I was told if I managed to keep a very hard jacket potato down I could go home. If a jacket potato is microwaved it should not be called a 'jacket potato' as it's not thick enough to be a jacket - It's more of a pashmina potato.

I couldn't keep it down, I knew something wasn't right but was discharged anyway. I couldn't breath properly, I had to pause for breath between each word I was saying. Mum and Joe called me 'Stevie' because they said I sounded like him off of Malcom in the Middle to which I'd laugh and say, "Yes. But. I. Really. Can't. Breath. Properly". After another, "Yes, it really is uncanny" from mum she thought it best to bring the doctor out again just in case.

Captain Poke-A-lot came out again and said something along the lines of, "Sweet lord have mercy, I think she's got pneumonia" and with that I was rushed back in to hospital. Actually getting back in the ward took ten hours though and mum was fuming with me because when we were about to be seen I'd wondered off to find a TV to watch Eastenders on. Eventually a nurse we saw not long after arrival spotted us and said to me, "Why aren't you on a ward yet, you're so ill?" We then got rushed in and I took a turn for the worse, needed to be hooked up to a breathing machine but one of the nurses didn't have her glasses on, didn't plug me in properly so I died again.

I couldn't remember the name of 'the breathing machine' and at one point put 'incubator' which made me laugh as that's what the babies are kept in isn't it? Had visions of a couple going to see their baby for the first time and there I am, "PICK ME! PICK ME!"

The X-Ray of my chest was fascinating - It was so foggy so impossible make out any organs and painful; I had to lie at an awkward and specific angle so found it hard to breath, sleep and be comfortable in any way but was still trying to get friends to take me out for a spliff, I was definitely trying to prolong the time I was in there as I felt safe.

I loved the routine and people. One day a new girl called Harriet came wheeling on in, "This town ain't big enough for the both of us" (*two Harriet's*) so I changed her name to, 'Hoona' on the board above her bed. She got upset because she was in for an eating disorder and thought it sounded like 'Heifer' which was definitely not my intention, it was just the first word I thought of that also began with H.

She had a talking Bagpuss toy but the batteries were running out on it because she'd lie on it in the night and I'd hear a garbled creep of a wheeze from it splutter, "I love cuddling little girls" which well and truly gave me the willies in the early hours.

She was really ill: nurses would bring her a meal and she'd have a panic attack, seeing someone hyperventilate from just the sight of food coming towards them was sad to see. In the end she was taken to a more specialist place in London.

When she left an awful smell started to rear itself, it turned out she'd been hiding food under my bed. For ages I was sat on my bed going, "What on earth is that smell?" Unbeknown to me I was like, 'The Princess and the Pea' but a more carnivorous version as I was above a mound of rotting ham sandwiches.

I saw her years later out clubbing and she still didn't look well. I was pissed, trying to help but drunken logic was all, "Let me get you a massive burger after this" which was a really stupid and thoughtless thing to say. I drunkenly saw the problem as this 'girl needs food immediately' rather than all the psychology behind it that had gone on for such a large chunk of her life. Here I am wanting more understanding of mental illness from people when even I've failed miserably in this instance.

Unsurprisingly she didn't take me up on the offer and didn't want to chat much after that which I totally get. Obviously I would never dream of saying anything like that now. I think of her from time to time and hope she's ok. I'll occasionally try and find her on Facebook but don't have a clue what her surname is. If anyone reading this knows a Hoona, please tell her to get in touch.

Reece and Jonny were the absolute best! I'd wake up every morning to Jonny wheeling himself in my bay in his wheelchair with a cup of tea for me sloshing around all over the shop. He was in there because he woke up one day and couldn't use his legs anymore, no-one had a clue what was causing it. I heard someone say it was all in his head which is mad isn't it if psychological? Others suggested he was putting it on but there was no way as I witnessed his physiotherapy sessions and the frustration and helplessness he clearly felt when he physically couldn't do the steps he wanted was undeniable. I'm pretty sure he was like that for two or three years and then one day as quick as it went, it suddenly came back.

Reece was the cooler one, quite charming, very mischievous. We'd go to the canteen at midnight with whichever of the nurses that would entertain our need for adventure.

Reece asked me to come in the room with him whilst he had his tablets one day, I did and it definitely wasn't what I thought it'd entail. I thought we'd go in, he'd take his tablets by putting them in his mouth and swallowing and that'd be that but oh no: we went in, he lay down, he looked really nervous, I held his hand, he had a dressing on his chest which a nurse peeled back and there was big hole in his chest where they put these tablets in so they'd dissolve and then they covered it all back up again. No wonder he looked nervous, poor chap! He's another one that I'd love to be friends with on Facebook, all this socialising came about before Facebook was a proper thing. I was more of a Myspace person, I remember having a cigarette with a girl outside a pub once and she was saying,

"Facebook's going to take over and be the only social network we use"

"No way! Facebook's boring as fuck, you can do so much more with Myspace"

Then it seemed over night that Myspace was no more. Has anyone checked on Tom? I hope he's ok.

Another of life's special ones was 'Hummingbird' she had something very wrong with her stomach, half of it seemed to be in a bag attached to her. Being in and out of hospital sadly was her life then and I do believe still is, the quality of it dictated by her stomach. Being well really is a blessing, it says something about her that despite it she still remains a none bitter legend.

13.) Institutionalised

When I came out of hospital for good I fucking hated it, I wanted to go back in so badly. I'd gotten used to the artificial lighting, I found the new natural glow and noise of birds tweeting went right through me. The outside world was too big and overwhelming, I missed the nurses, my new friends, the routine and the children's ward in general.

I'd been given lots of tablets to be getting on with, I couldn't shake the feeling of not wanting to be back in this existence so one evening when I was watching a Hollyoaks late night episode where Lewis Richardson (programme baddie) was taking his own life with tablets and vodka I decided to join him but I didn't have any vodka and because I'm an idiot I decided to replace it with fabric softener. It was a Bold move.

I obviously did it just to get back into hospital which backfired because since I'd gotten out I'd had my eighteenth birthday so wasn't allowed in the children's ward anymore. The adult ward was horrible, the opposite to what the children's ward was - I was left in a trolley over night surrounded by all sorts of carnage, the nurses were different with me, it was clear they saw me as "just another time waster" now. A doctor tried to talk to me to get me to go to the psychiatric ward for further assessment but I just ran away screaming, "I am not crazy" which perhaps didn't help my cause. Especially with my gown open at the back and my arse hanging out.

I get that the NHS are understaffed so it'd be easier for them if people didn't take drugs or whatever to get themselves admitted but no-one of a completely sound mind is at that stage and I think that really needs to be taken in to account. I recently met a homeless lady who clearly needed to go to the hospital as she had septicaemia but she didn't want to go because they treat her like shit there. When did that become a thing? Honestly, the way in which we treat the homeless in the UK is disgusting, when did we forget that they're humans like us? They've clearly just had a series of unfortunate occurrences that have led them there which could happen to any of us, except perhaps some rich which is perhaps why they look at them with the most disdain.

Nevertheless that hospital trip was a wakeup call, I knew I wanted better for myself. My parents definitely installed something in me because whatever state I've been in mentally there's always still been a feeling of ambition and drive rumbling deep within my gusset, even if it was at its most faintest in the before mentioned tale.

14.) College take two

I got myself ready to go back to college. Since I'd been away dying a new course had been developed a B-TEC in Drama and Performance which was mainly practical of which I was most chuffed about. The tutor was a weasel of a man, I was going to say he was clearly going through sort of a midlife crisis but feel that'd be excusing his behaviour. He had an old sports car that was similar to that of Batman's (the first one) his hair was dyed a strange rusty orange colour, it of course was all spiked up and he only ever seemed to have time for the prettiest girls in the class.

I was clearly not a joy to deal with at this point though, but again there were clearly issues and any good teacher would've noticed this.

The abuse was still ongoing, he was still very much alive and even with the joyful interlude of hospital I was so very alone, even more now actually as lovely people like Kelly and Holly had skedaddled away to university. I was covering everything up with alcohol, bottle after bottle of gin. It got to the point where often I wasn't even getting drunk any more, just always topping up.

I partied hard at college. Most in my new class were a couple of years younger than me and I don't think of myself as particularly mature but by this point I'd already experienced such a lot so there was just no common ground.

One girl Mindy was the same age as me, she'd moved to Cornwall from London. I was ranting and raving about everyone to her after they'd been particularly annoying in a lesson.

One girl in the class I met as I was walking by and noticed her coughing up something in a bush, I asked if she was all right and she laughed and said it was cum from a married guy she'd been sucking off for breakfast. There's an awful lot to take in there isn't there? (*Pardon the pun*) For that I'm sorry.

THEN in the lesson the same girl came up to me, got the ruler out of my pencil-case and started to show me on it how big said married mans appendage was. I'm definitely not easily shocked but was absolutely dumbfounded by this behaviour so was expressing this to Mindy who seemed to find it all very funny and quickly we became close friends.

Mindy was living with an old family friend in the middle of nowhere and found it boring so started staying at mine most nights. She got on really well with mum too, there was a buzz in the house again that had been dormant since dad left.

I thought of her like a sister at one point so of course I opened up to her which I guess then became the problem in our relationship. She was quite controlling and this was another thing she thought she could control. I'd by now been to the police but they were useless and made me feel like it was all my fault. I offered to set up a place and a time for them to catch MC in action to which they agreed then failed to show up.

Mindy said if she wasn't part of the solution she was part of the problem but her only solution was the police and when I'd express it wasn't a route I wanted to go down again she'd act like I was being difficult, that I was happy with what my life had become. Friendships were my sanctuary, I didn't need someone to turn up, assume they knew how everything was then let me know that if I don't do what they think I should do even though I'd already tried it then they "couldn't be friends with me anymore."

Mindy fancied a toxic guy I'd known most of my life (another one). I first became aware of this one when he broke in to my garage when I was about nine or ten and stole my bicycle. We knew it was him because that's the sort of thing he was already renowned for doing so when his dad miraculously "just found it" in his garden there was no way it was a coincidence.

I knew of two woman that had fallen asleep at parties and woke up to him having sex with them, raping them.

If I know that's happened to two women, how many more has that happened too?

Mindy grew fond of this absolute catch, she'd waste hours chatting to him on nights out and I'd be pissed sauntering past shouting "You dirty raping bike thief bastard!" Mindy snapped one day,

"I asked him and he said he didn't do it."
"Oh, because rapist thieves are renowned for their honesty."

They eventually got together, she said his dick was curly like a pigs and it was then she had nothing more to do with him. She could make peace with the fact he was a rapist and a thief but having a dick like a farmyard animal was one step too far.

15.) All hail, Spangle

Mindy went out with another guy who was and still is an absolute legend, by far the best thing about her was meeting him. Spangle was an absolute character, didn't give a fuck, loved to smoke weed and party and I for one at that time was a fan of all the above. On a deeper level, his childhood was pretty shambolic so he got used to his friends being more like his family from such a young age so whenever you were around him and his friends it always felt special… well, like a family.

Mindy moved in with Spangle far too quickly and I wanted to spend all my time there as there was never any judgement from him. Before long though the cracks in their relationship started to show, Spangle could not be moulded, he couldn't be any other way than how he was.

Spangle's dad was the local mayor which wasn't a good thing as there was no sense of accountability because whatever he did his dad would get him out of it because he felt guilty for walking out on his family years previous.

Mindy used to get Spangle to secretly follow me home to make sure I was safe which was actually really lovely of her. MC would always know though and save the repercussions for when I didn't have a chaperone.

16.) Mystic Meg

I had a dream (all right Martin) where I fell out
with everyone on a night out and ended up going home
early but on the way home a guy (someone different to
MC) attacked me so badly that I was in intensive care
and didn't make it through the night. Then one night
(in real life) I did a load of magic mushrooms and
everything in that dream started to come true. The
same conversations started happening so I'd skirt
around the bits that would lead to us falling out but
what I didn't factor in was that I was now coming up
from all these magic mushrooms whilst in a busy folk
pub with wood chipping on the floor that had started
to turn different colours and my arms started to
float above my head. I suddenly didn't trust anyone,
especially my friends. My head was absolutely mashed
anyway without bringing psychedelics into it.

I felt everything was closing in on me, I needed to
get out immediately so ran out with my arms still in
the air. I thought I saw the man in my dream up ahead
and then a purple dog appeared so I followed it into
a bush made out of sardines and stayed there crying
for about six hours. When exiting the bush I found I
had a lot of missed calls from Mindy, our friendship
had already become strained without this extra layer.

She was furious with me, had assumed something awful had happened and it would be down to her to let my mum know. She didn't want to see me for a bit.

Trying to escape reality was not working out too well either.

I remember cycling to Saffie's thinking I could perhaps get a bit of friendship from her but she'd become friends with Mindy by now, Mindy had obviously discussed everything with her and it would seem she shared the same sentiment as upon arrival I could feel the awful atmosphere radiating from her too.

17.) A dalliance with a cast member from Eastenders

I did magic mushrooms once more, this time with Spangle, indoors. I was curled up on a sofa with a fire blazing (I think this fire might have only existed in my head.) I thought I was a cat, just meowing away: the only problem was when the mushrooms wore off I'd forgotten how to speak human and was still 'speaking cat' for a day after.

Mindy left Spangle which resulted in their house turning into some kind of squat, it was an absolute mess but I loved it.

We went to a barn dance rave and I took so many drugs it's a wonder I was still alive. I bumped into a friend's dad who gave me a wrap of speed, I took that then stumbled into a field with all these giant papier-mâché animals. I wanted to sit on top of the donkey but went to do so at such velocity that I put my foot through its side and got stuck.

Everyone seemed to be in the other fields and no matter how much I sang no-one came to my rescue; although I'm not sure why I didn't just try regular shouting.

My exit strategy was inspired by the Fosbury Flop, I hoofed myself back so vigorously that I fell off and landed with my ankle twisted around a bail of hay. It looked at least sprained as it resembled a lump of fat black gammon.

I must've hitched a lift soon after because I ended up miles away but nearer home so popped to the garage for a Pot Noodle. As I was hobbling, gurning, dribbling, Pot Noodle-ing my way home, the police pulled up because they thought I was a missing person.

"But I'm here" I exclaimed.

The officer asked for ID, "Hold this" I said, handing him my Pot Noodle as I searched. I only had my fake ID from when I was underage, 'Lucinda Minnow' it read. The officer oddly accepted this as fine and off he went.

Once back home, due to not being in a good place mentally and all the drugs I'd taken, I'd convinced myself it was only a matter of time until the police realised I was not Lucinda Minnow, they'd tell the government (because that's clearly a government matter) then the government would "come after me." There was only one thing for it: I would have to go on the run.

I had an on-the-run outfit which consisted of a green wooly hat, Ozzy Osbourne sunglasses, Dr Martens, green chinos and a shirt with a frill, because nothing says on the run like an Edwardian ruff.

My first port of call was the bank, I had no money but an overdraft, somehow managed to take out 1K and put £500 in each back pocket.

My style of walking was to drag one leg behind, like the guy out of the film, 'The Usual Suspects' so even though I felt I was making a good distance, I definitely wasn't. I headed up a hill that would take me away from the city but as I started I heard a police siren which panicked me into thinking I needed to be the on opposite side to where I was. The problem being the opposite side had a river between.

As another siren sounded I saw the tide was out and made the bold decision to "run" across. Ten steps in and I was neck deep in mud, I looked like 'The Head' from Art Attack.

I figured, "Well I guess this is my life now" and started singing to comfort myself. My song of choice was, 'Professional Widow' by Tori Amos.

My actions caused more commotion than I realised because before long the fire brigade came whirring away to hoof me out.

It took four firefighters to pull me out. Once sufficiently loosened, I shot out in such a way that all the money in my back pockets flew out and fluttered through the air. I looked like a shit Cornish piñata.

I grabbed what money I could and was hoisted to safety, a firefighter put her arm around me, I lifted it off and hobble-ran away as fast as I could - After all I was on the run.

Swampy I looked so headed to Peacocks for a costume change. There was a ridiculous amount of leopard print in store but that suited me fine because I was at my most manic and had decided that up until now I'd been living a lie. I was not Harriet Dyer but in fact Kat Slater from Eastenders, everything that had happened thus far had led me to this moment.

Whilst I paid for my leopard paraphernalia the woman at the counter was giving me awful looks as I'd traipsed mud everywhere, then slopped a load of caked in mud money on top of the counter. I felt she was stifling me so ordered her to "Get out of my pub" which I'm sure was more Peggy Mitchell than Kat Slater but accuracy by this point was a distant memory.

Being on the run must've become further from my mind because I then just went to the pub. A pub where it was always £1 for a bottle of Carlsberg, "I'll get a round in… for myself."

A whole scene was playing out, but of course it was my brain malfunctioning. I thought I saw Zoe Slater

(Kat's secret daughter at that time) so was screaming, "I'm your muvvvaaaaaa" at this poor bewildered girl that was on a trial shift. Then I thought I saw Alfie Moon (Kat's love interest in Eastenders) so followed that poor guy around that actually didn't look anything like him.

"Alfie" was on a break from work, he tried to shake me off but I hid then followed him back to work and waited for him outside whilst drinking drinks I'd stolen off a table at the pub. I waved at him through the window, I thought sexily but it must have been a horrific sight.

I'll always be grateful to that chap for how he was with me that day, he didn't call the police and after work instead of running away he brought me a pasty and we sat on a bench and had a chat. After a couple of hours I realised I probably wasn't Kat Slater after all and he most definitely wasn't Alfie Moon. All of this was quite the pickle so off home I went for a cuddle from mum and a long sleep.

I slept for two days and awoke to numerous missed calls, general panic and chaos. One thing I learnt was I had a part in a play where I had to abseil down the side of a theatre, I sprung up and went in the bathroom to have a shower and clean my teeth. You know those metal strips with screws in that are where the bathroom ends and the hall way begins? One of those screws was slightly raised, the floor was wet, I was in a hurry and slipped on the Lino slicing my foot open. My foot was a flappy bloody mess but I did not have the time to deal with it so put my shoes on and off I went.

I got to the theatre, signed in, got hooked up to abseil, got hoisted to the top, my shoe had now filled up with blood and was dripping on people below and down the side of the wall so got hoisted back down and sent to hospital where all that was mopped up and then a dressing was put on. It was my black gammon leg they paid more attention to, apparently I'd quite seriously chipped a bone, they wanted to put a cast on it,

"Absolutely not, I'm off raving later."

18.) A calming influence

At college I had to work with a girl called Lucy, we were each others understudies for our adaptation of Shakespeare's, A Comedy of Errors. After the intensity with Mindy I was glad of her company: she was kind, calm, easy going and fun. She most definitely hadn't been tainted by the world yet and that was what I needed, someone that still saw things purely.

I hope people wouldn't say I led Lucy astray because I don't think I did, we had some great nights out, she'd come to mine every Monday after college and we'd go to the local nightclub where the dress code was "Wear a smile" for Hip Hop Mondays. Every week it'd be the exact same playlist because only a certain amount of Hip Hop seemed to have made its way to Cornwall.

One night I'd convinced myself that vodka jelly shots were illegal so was getting them from the bar and then smuggling them up my jumper to the toilets in order to eat them in private. The same night there was a poor guy playing pool with his friend that I decided just by looking at him that he was a pedophile so started shouting this at him. At one point he turned to me and said, "You seem like a nice person, I don't know why you're doing this" to which

I screamed, "PEDOPHILE!" and started putting his pool balls in my pockets. Before long the bouncers came to accost me but I hid behind the table and started to throw the balls at their heads.

That's how you get kicked out and banned for a month.

Raising the question: What would you have to do to be banned for life?

College attendance for Tuesday mornings was none existent. I was told there was to be an assessment the Tuesday morning after the Monday night I was allowed back in the club and if I didn't pass I'd get kicked off the course.

This shocked me into "adjusting" my ways. I still went out, got hammered but then stayed up until 6am learning the script. The script was about a woman wanking a guy off in a cinema that turned out to be her son, it was so fucked up that it kept me interested enough to get it done. I passed with flying colours. I'm one of those people that if someone thinks I can't do something or starts to write me off I'll make sure I prove them wrong which is all well and good but would be far easier if I didn't behave in a way where anyone would need to think about writing me off in the first place.

In the final year of college we all went on a trip first to Gibraltar and then to Spain with our adaptation of Comedy of Errors and were doing workshops in schools too. I'm not sure how it happened but half of us had acquired mumps before the trip so it was uncertain if we'd even be allowed to go.

I'd done so well not to get it but had a madness fuelled night out the night before the trip and when I'd woken up the next day, the mumps had struck. There'd also been a terrible smell but that wasn't anything to do with mumps - I'd put a burger in each back pocket at the end of the night in order to be allowed on the bus home but had forgotten about them and after sitting on them for the 45 minute bus journey they had become deeply embedded in my trouser fabric.

I'd never flown before so was really nervous, Lucy held my hand. An air hostess offered us a glass of orange juice each on a tray but I got confused and tried to take the whole tray from her.

At the airport I'd seen our tutor, Monsieur Weasel buying condoms which was unnerving because he was catching up with a girl in Spain he'd met the previous year that must've been around the same age as us, his students.

I'd come to expect this sort of behaviour from men which sadly is why they get away with it. At secondary school there was a science teacher in his 40's seeing a student (bearing in mind everyone's 16 and under). Our history teacher was known for looking up girls skirts, everyone knew, we worryingly saw it as, "Just what he did." Also my science teacher used to walk me home from time to time, he'd tell me I was different to the other kids and in my year book he wrote, "Keep wearing those pretty earrings of yours" I thought he was so kind but now looking back, I don't think that was quite right either. Less focus on my jewellery, more on your bunsen burners please Mr Leicester.

19.) So very calm

The first night in Gibraltar, I'd been drinking, was tired, had mumps, fell out with anyone, "Fuck this and fuck all of you, I'm going home" I shouted and tried to fly home, with my arms.

There was a teacher who was another hippy type that'd project she cared when really she didn't give a shit. She was trying to calm me down but everything she was saying was so insincere. She had to sleep in the same room as me so I didn't sneak off to punch anyone, it was clear she wanted to be anywhere but there. There was always so much rage inside me. I remember her saying a one point, "You've got fire in your eyes, I'm not sure what more I can do, you might need exorcising."

The next day Monsieur Weasel gave me a warning, I was told if I got two more I'd be sent home. The second night I got another because I was smoking on the roof of where we were staying. I didn't understand what the problem was, I was doing them a favour going outside!

I liked Gibraltar, even after a monkey had shat on my head. Twenty cigarettes were less than a quid and a litre of gin was less than three quid, I was in heaven. A load of girls got pissed and went back to an army base with some guys on the third night which took the heat off me.

Another night we were in a pub and a girl was chatting with a guy, the vibes I got from him were, 'Massive Prick.' She went to the toilet and the guy went after her, she was gone for a bit and it didn't sit right with me so I expressed my concerns to the group but they assured me there was nothing to worry about. My gut said otherwise so I went after her, pushed each cubicle door open, one slammed shut with such force and then I heard a whimper. I was furious, was not going to let this happen, we were on our holidays! I started shouting, she's saying he won't let her go. "Not on my watch pal" I scaled the door, the fire must've been back in my eyes because the moment I was over and looked at him he left, the little cretin. BE VIGILANT GIRLS! No-one else had anything to lose by checking to see if she was all right.

That night we went clubbing, I went to the toilet, heard a little yelp and was on high alert so scaled another door to find a very tiny girl standing on the toilet because a pipe or something had burst and she was surrounded by shit. I picked her up and on the way out of the toilets I saw a guy that was so handsome. I was pissed, brave, abroad and I guess eager for a none traumatic sexual experience. I do believe I did a most out of order move and pinched him on the bottom. To my surprise he seemed interested so off we went for a bit of "how's your father" (PLEASE DON'T BRING MY DAD INTO THIS) up the Gibraltar rock. Encounters like this are always so anticlimactic, once there I felt out of my depth. He was most well endowed and it would barely fit anywhere so it was quite an uncomfortable experience. He seemed quite nice though so we had a pleasant chat and he held my hand as we walked back, to my surprise at the bottom of the rock was the hippy teacher looking for me with the fire now in her eyes. Off I was frog marched back to where we were staying and informed of my final strike.

They started slapping these curfews on me (I should've been sent home, but I don't think they envisaged I would actually get a third strike) I'd have to sneak around to get pissed. Monsieur Weasel was on a rampage looking for me to get me back in my room but the lovely girls I was with (Lucy and her friends) heard him coming so shoved me under a bed in their room so I wouldn't get in trouble. Hearing them fob him off really made me feel warm inside. The only downside was for some reason there was a load of fried chicken under the bed so in my haste I'd face planted a bargain bucket, which meant I was now warm on the outside too. Oh how we laughed.

We headed to Spain, on the first night a girl got pickpocket, had all of her money and passport taken so Lucy and an other girl sprinted after the robbers. At least a mile in to the chase they came across a policeman who seemed to be in cahoots with the culprits as Lucy could see them hiding in the police car whilst they were saying they hadn't seen them which was strange.

The girl that idiot tried to trap in the toilets had grandparents that lived in Spain and she chose a few of us to go spend the day with them, she chose me and I was so flattered as it was the nicest of days. Her grandparents were lovely, welcoming and their home had a swimming pool! The spread they put on was delicious too, I felt like royalty lounging by the pool, hanging out with absolute legends and eating like Queens whilst everyone else was off spending the day being led around by Monsieur Weasel and the bell-ends (great name for a band).

I always seem to get on well with peoples grandparents. When I was ten I went to a birthday party in a water park (but it's a Cornish water park so just a wave machine, an actual outdoor playground slide and a load of plasters floating by) we all went back to his house after and as the other kids mucked around and played games I sat with his grandparents. We drank tea and chatted about, 'The good old days.'

After the dalliance with the chap on Gibraltar rock I was washing my bikini bottoms out in a sink one morning, his appendage was so large it had made me bleed a bit. A girl asked what I was doing, I told her and she helped me wash them which was nice of her. I tried thanking her again that night and she stopped me in my tracks saying, "I don't want to talk about that." That was the thing, no-one wanted to about anything that wasn't sweetness and light which leads to repression which then leads to bubbling and spewing of same repression. If cyphered out gradually would've been far less of an issue.

All bikini bottom washer needed to say was, "No worries mate" and that would've been that. She could've even thrown a, "Hope you're all right" in there too, heaven forbid.

My mum's dear friend Liz once told me that the thing she loved most about my mum was that she could always be exactly how she is and my mum loved her for that and that's what a friend said to me once, she loves that I don't judge so she can always be herself. I found that lovely but also think it should be a given with friends.

We got the coach back to Cornwall. It baffled me how people can sleep sitting down, I have to be flat. I said to everyone on the way back, "Bagsy sleeping in the aisle on the coach" but everyone responded with, "No-one else wants to do that Harriet."

One girl fell asleep with her music on so loud that you could hear ever word to every song she was playing crystal clear. She was playing the song 'Locked Up' by Akon on a loop then fell asleep with that same song repeating itself for pretty much the whole journey.

By the time it stopped Akon had gotten out.

We arrived back at college, went home to sleep then met up that evening to watch Mean Girls at the cinema and as it was Monday we all went clubbing after which was especially fun with post holiday giddiness.

Apparently no-one went abroad as part of the course again because of our behaviour. In hindsight I should've treated it less like an 18-30's holiday.

20.) Free from the shackles of education

Spangle and I hung out with a guy that sold drugs. He seemed like a prick at first, he said I was very nosey as I asked him questions about when he went out with a girl I went to school with but I thought I was just making conversation. He had people after him because he owed so much money because instead of selling the drugs he ate the drugs. His business plan was definitely flawed.

He decided to deal with this in quite a questionable manner, he had 100 ecstasy tablets, a last ditch attempt to make money to pay off some of what he owed but instead decided that him, Spangle, I and a couple of comers and goers would take them all in a few days. To assist with this fool proof plan we also got a ridiculous amount of weed and probably hundreds of little stubby beers in.

We were a mess. I remember not eating for nutrition but because the drugs needed something to feed off. I had a part-time teaching drama job at a local theatre on the Sunday and remember the woman's face when she let me in after that week, she was aghast.

The soundtrack to those times was The Streets album, 'Original Pirate Material' what an album, even now if

I hear it I think of those times. To others this may seem like just more destructive times but I loved them, I felt so safe and loved with those boys. We were similar, all a bit lost and broken but overall were good eggs.

I needed money to fund this lifestyle, I needed a job. Those days it wasn't accepted to have piercings in a work place so I was turned down from many places just for that. Although now I'm thinking of it perhaps my constant aroma of gin and weed might have had something to do with it too.

I had a job interview at TK Maxx, I got very stoned beforehand but bizarrely it couldn't have gone better. My parents had introduced me to the Plymouth TK Maxx years before and I absolutely loved it. Designer brands and bargain prices? Yes please.

When I was asked in the interview if I ever shopped there I replied, "DO I? My shoes are from TK Maxx, my shirt's from TK Maxx, my trousers…" you get the picture. I was told they'd never seen someone so enthusiastic about TK Maxx. Good job I was stoned, I might've been a bit too much otherwise.

I worked with one girl, Lisa who was really nice. She asked if I could cover her fitting room shift whilst she went to lunch because her mum was meeting her.

"Of course"
"Oh look, here she is now!"

I couldn't believe it, there coming up the escalator was the woman that used to jump out of a bush at me on the way to school with a bottle of vodka in her hand and a wonky wig, I almost didn't recognise her as this woman was holding a Capri-sun. Whatever you do, don't squeeze it!

Lisa had a lot to deal with, from the sounds of it they had to drag themselves up. Lisa had to raise her younger sister Soriah because well, their mother was busy living in a bush. Her sister used to come in to visit, there was something really special about her, it sounds wanky but she had a brilliant energy about her and because I had a vague idea of what she'd been through I wanted to help her. Lisa asked me to have a word with her a couple of times because for some reason she looked up to me, she'd make me think she was really taking on board what I said but it was all out the other ear the moment we departed ways.

I bumped in to Soriah with one of her pals during a night out once, it was pretty obvious they were off their tits on pills which was concerning because she must've only been in her early teens. I asked if she was ok and if she needed anything but she said she was having the best time and she just wanted a cuddle. That I could do and off they excitedly scurried.

She started to prefer sleeping on the streets as oppose to being at her sisters which I found strange.

One night I left the club, passed an alleyway on the way home and heard sobbing, I peeked in and there she was crying and planning to sleep there. "Come along now, you're coming to mine."

It was a Saturday night so my mum had a chicken out on the side to defrost for dinner the next day, I went upstairs to get her some pyjama's, came back down and she was trying to eat my mums frozen chicken. "What the bloody heck have you taken?"

Other than that she was an absolute joy as usual but once I tried to delve in to what was going on it was nods and smiles, again just saying what she thought I wanted to hear. She left before my mum got up for work with the pyjamas and duvet I gave her all folded up in a neat pile, with the chicken on top.

Her and Ray (the badass kid from school with a penchant for squids) got together, of course they did, two broken souls, they had a baby. I hoped it would sort the pair of them out but it didn't. Remember the person that got their kid taken away because they left them with a group of swans? Yes, you guessed it.

It seems chicken is a gateway bird.

New people started to join my social group, they were ok but not like Spangle and I and as a result the dynamic started to shift. Remember Bill, the guy that dumped me on Valentine's Day because he was jealous of the kid with cerebral palsy? He turned up at the pub one day smoking like he was Danny Zuko, but not actually inhaling. He was an A* student at school destined for the biggest of things but now here he was pretending to be someone he most definitely was not. He got bored of achieving, dropped out of uni and now seemed to be the male version of 'Deborah, Deborah' in Pulp's Common People song.

He brought with him his female equivalent, 'Deborah' then I guess? They were both going out with other people but were cheating on them with each other, which is a perfect depiction of the people they were. They were dead behind the eyes, which you usually get with people that have taken too many drugs of which I don't think they had yet, they must've had no souls to begin with, but on the plus side were really well suited.

Deborah was yet another one of those people that'd be overly lovely but was once again projecting what she wanted you to think she was.

"Let's have a mad session tonight!"
"I'm a bit skint today so I best give it a miss"
"Oh don't you worry about that, I'll sort all your drugs out for nothing"
"Really? Nice one, thank you."

Then the next day as I woke she'd be in my face, "Right, you owe me this amount for this and that amount for that" and would present me with a bill.

It was so much less fun with them around and their chat was shit, it was all about chasing the best drugs whereas before it was being silly, laughing and of course having 'deep and meaningful's' because that's what you do at 4am when you're off your tits.

Even me and Spangle were drifting a tiny bit. Since his relationship with Mindy he'd become a fuck boy, and once he'd fucked himself around the whole of Cornwall he'd ended up in another relationship with a girl that was stunning but sadly that's where it ended (which is how it has to be otherwise the world would implode).

Any night out with them just ended up with them having horrible screaming rows with each other. It never looked fun. A group of us went to a dirty stinking club in Plymouth. I wasn't allowed in because I was wearing trainers, "This is no time for standards, there's a man injecting his toes behind you!"

There was a bowling alley nearby so I popped in there, swapped my shoes and then they let me in. I should never should have gone, I liked drugs but I was never fussed with the music that seemed to go with it plus drugs weren't my everything like they were with these people.

Hard house can do one! I'd rather be fucked up listening to Whitney. Plus doing drugs with a group of people you're disconnecting from is never a good thing.

We had to wait around once the club shut for the first train back home. We were roaming the streets for hours, gurning so much, I remember walking by someone eating a giant bag of Hula Hoops and each crunch felt like a mountain collapsing all within the confinements of my skull so I cowered back until I found my way behind a wall where I stayed until the train came.

Once on the train everyone was doing coke on the tables not caring about who was watching. We got back to the now squat and I had an epiphany, everyone was sitting around chatting and seemingly getting on but none of it was real, the drugs had overtaken, no-one was really paying attention to the chat, it was one eye at all times on who had the drugs and where they were going next.

I was done so got up, "I'm off"
"Will you be back?"
"No, I don't think I will" and I didn't, of course it was only Spangle that even noticed.

I went home and had a very painful roast dinner with my mum and brother, I'd been gurning so much that my mouth was riddled with ulcers. Ulcers mixed with piping hot gravy and scratchy stuffing was not a welcome combo.

I'd still go out with Lucy, she was a tonic. Once we were at a club called, 'The Twilight Zone' and saw a guy enter who she thought was "ansum" (which is Cornish speak for "what a beaut.")

Lucy was shy, I'd never known her to fancy anyone, she'd never been with anyone before too so whether right or wrong I gave her a little push and said, "If you get with him I'll give you a tenner." He "Tiger" turned out to be a fucking idiot, I regret to this day suggesting she get with him.

Lucy had a birthday, her family went all out and hired out a surf lodge in Newquay, we were all staying in the rooms there after the party. It was amazing, we were up until stupid 'o' clock drinking and dancing. Everyone started to retire to their rooms but Lucy and I were still at the bar drinking tequila - No beer mat was safe!

Eventually the bar closed, Lucy went to bed, it was just me up and I decided I needed another drink so snuck into the store cupboard, found a case of Becks, polished it all off then fell asleep cuddling the empty box.

The next day Lucy's dad was at the surf lodge's computer and called me over. There I was on the CCTV sneaking like Pink Panther, telling myself to shush whilst robbing them. I was mortified and very apologetic but luckily he saw the funny side so all was forgiven. That hangover the next day was one of

the worst I think I've ever had, it was that day too
that once up we went to the beach, I was standing up
looking around and a seagull flew in to my head and
knocked me unconscious.

21.) A very sad time

I was still clubbing most Mondays, this Monday in particular I bumped into dear school friend Thea, it was so good to see her. Everyone from the same group was still hanging out years later, the only one that wasn't really a part of it any more was me. Having said that when we did catch up it was exactly the same, she was such good company. That night Thea got me a drink as I'd run out of money so I said I'd get her one back the following Monday.

That weekend she was driving to her grandads house to deliver him a roast dinner with her boyfriend and little brother in the car, a freak hailstorm came from nowhere, the car skidded, crashed and she died. Her boyfriend was in intensive care and her little brother broke his leg but was awake for it all.

Next Monday never came.

When anyone passes away you always hear in the news someone that knew them saying, "They were such a beautiful person" but she was the most, it's still incomprehensible sixteen years later. The world definitely became a worse place when she left it. She was her parents world too, to see them since, they are empty shells of the people they once were, so heartbreaking.

I found it unjust that I was still stuck on this planet in a miserable existence and her, someone who brought so much pleasure to so many people was not. That being said though, it was how it was and I guess a wake-up call, that it could all be over at any second and is up to me and me only to change my miserable existence.

22.) Sayonara Cornwall

I needed to get out of Cornwall, too much had happened there for me to ever be truly happy. I didn't have the money to just leave so figured the only way to do it would be through the educational route. The only thing I enjoyed was performing / acting so that's what I'd do. Drama school was always the dream for me and that's what my peers were getting ready to do, but they were doing it with their families footing the bill. Another advantage they had was they looked like they could be moulded in to whatever the schools wanted them to be whereas I was this smoking, drinking, covered in piercings loose cannon.

The drama school, East 15 seemed to 'get me' the most. I could be myself, it was definitely the least pretentious one I auditioned for. Even that didn't work out in the end though because my voice wasn't up to scratch. I was a dick, was smoking a lot and would get myself so worked up with nerves and anxiety before every audition that my throat and voice would suffer.

The best part about traipsing all over the country for drama school auditions was dad and I were starting to bond again as he always loved theatre and the arts so wanted to take me which was good of him. Before this it had been fraught, if he'd of just said something along the lines of, "Do you know what, I love your mum, she's such a wonderful woman and I really do respect her but I've had these feelings all my life which I've been trying to come to terms with that manifested in a way that in hindsight was destructive and ended up hurting the people that love me the most" we'd have been able to move past all the eggy-ness far sooner.

Even now I don't think we've had a proper chat about it all, perhaps it is odd and some people might think, "No parent should have to ever talk to their kid about their sexual preferences!" I agree, but if said sexual preferences has essentially derailed your whole family then we probably do.

We were once coming back from a drama school audition on the sleeper train from London and we had a few gins before bed and he sort of half explained / half apologised in his own way and I was grateful for that.

There was one drama schools that was proper interested in me but I'm not even sure if it was legit. I can't even remember what it was called now but it definitely had the word 'science' in the title which doesn't bode well and I distinctively remember it being next door to a prison. Still the fees were ridiculous and there were no scholarships, there was no way my family and I could muster that kind of money.

University seemed to be the logical option, one that had a practical based drama degree. I went to a taster day at Wolverhampton University and didn't find it good, I left thinking the college I'd attended had far better facilities when surely it should be the other way around.

Lucy said she was going to Wolverhampton University. "Then that my friend is where we shall go!"

I had just under a year to save so picked up as many shifts as possible at TK Maxx. I liked my boss but she was quite vacuous and shallow, she didn't seem to have any friends or indeed much of a life out of work and was obsessed with how she looked, especially tanning. Once she was sunbathing on the roof, the door slammed behind her and she was stuck up there for just under 24 hours and no-one noticed she was missing.

Her one true love was her sausage dog, one day because she'd learnt her lesson she was off to an actual sun bed shop, she asked me if I could look after her dog for her while she was gone then gave me a paper towel to put on my finger and said,

"If the dogs bowel comes out of its bum just pop it back in gently."

"I'm not sure that's part of my job description Pamela."

I got on well with the lady that worked in the cash office at TK Maxx, well I thought I did but she said something that stuck with me. There were two of us counting down the days until we left for Uni and she said specifically to me, "You won't see it through, you'll be back here within six months." I felt she didn't know me but obviously I didn't know for sure and started to doubt myself. This was my one chance to leave and hopefully make something of my life.
When I did find things hard and contemplate giving up, her saying that would pop in my head and spur me on. Perhaps because I was the first to make jokes and liked a drink a lot people mistook that as stupidity or an inability to take anything seriously so always had such low expectations of me. The other girl did quit uni and return to Cornwall after six months.

The day finally came for us to head to University. Lucys' family were so good to me, as no-one in my family had a car they took me and moved me in. I stayed at theirs the night before so we could set off at 6am. I had all of my possessions in one massive suitcase, I thought Lucy had the same but that was just for jewellery, she hadn't packed the rest yet! Her dad had a truck which was exciting to trundle up the motorway in, both her parents came. Once we were moved in, they took us for lunch which was kind of them, they made me feel I was part of their family.

We instantly had an advantage as everyone else had to start the experience on their own, we didn't know anyone else but it was never a problem because we had each other. As it happened though we did make other friends quickly too, I think because we always had so much fun together so it was infectious. We loved dancing like idiots, by day one I'd acquired the nickname, "Crazy Legs."

Even though all my lessons were in Wolverhampton, I chose to stay in the Walsall campus. "Why did you choose to do that Harriet, it sounds like quite the inconvenience?" I chose where I lived based on where had the most security and where Lucy was so Walsall's where I ended up, I'd get the bus in to Wolverhampton for lessons. One of the best decisions I ever made.

Everyone on my course bar two people were insufferable. I'd had time off with hospital / year out to save etc so was now almost five years older than the others on my course and even for that age they were young acting and this was the first time they were 'living life' really whereas I'd already had a life, of sorts. They were the sort of people that'd suggest spin the bottle at a party and would arrive at said party shouting, "The party's arrived!"

The other halls of residence were not nice at all, I wouldn't have felt safe or comfortable living there. Where I was living was a little village new build with my own toilet, I instantly fell in love with it.

Just as I was really starting to enjoy our new surroundings, Lucy's now boyfriend Tiger turned up, totally out of the blue having driven up from Cornwall through the night, he arrived as we were getting in from a night out, I thought I was hallucinating. He told no-one of his plans, just secretly enrolled then turned up and sure enough the big wanker had taken all the same courses as Lucy AND ME so I'd be seeing him regularly. Lord give me strength.

Since meeting that time they'd become inseparable. I liked him at first, I always feel a kinship with people that have been through stuff, he was brought up by in foster care because his mum was an alcoholic that used to sporadically turn up at school and try to kidnap him. I really felt for him until I realised he dined out on it, it was his automatic go to excuse for his awful behaviour. He was the first person Lucy had been with so she was completely blind to how he really was, she definitely had a severe case of the dick mist. This was another reason I saw uni as a good thing, I thought being around new people she'd find someone that would treat her how she should be treated but that wasn't going to happen now.

Before long Lucy got the nickname 'Batty.' She asked Tiger to buy her this pair of sparkly red high heels shoes.

"Of course, as long as you let me put my willy up you bum."

"Absolutely not, you scoundrel!" Then the next day she was tottering around in these red shoes so we were all like, "Mmmmmm Batty!"

Tiger had bizarrely never seen a black person before and would stare at the black girls during our classes. Once he stared at this girl solidly then grabbed her shoe and threw it out the window - We were up six floors, it could've decapitated someone. Luckily they'd never met anyone like him either so weren't as offended as they should've been, everyone just found each other fascinating. Their idea of what Cornwall was surprised me too, one girl asked me if we have roads. No Clarissa, and we all live up trees.

23.) A light upon the horizon

I quickly realised that it was all very well leaving Cornwall but wherever you go your brain is still in your head. I was drinking too much, still had the trauma I hadn't dealt with but now had the added bonus of missing my mum like nothing I'd ever felt too.

I wasn't going to lessons, I always felt suicidal which was rearing it's ugly head at the end of nights out to people I didn't even know. Then a game changer occurred, my university was the only one in the country at the time to have a module in stand-up comedy, something which I had no idea about.

No-one in my class would work with me due to me either not turning up or turning up with an Evian bottle filled with gin, which upon reflection is actually fair enough.

There were a few I got bunched with on account of them being just a run up from me in terms of people not wanting to work with them. Our sense of humour was in no way matched though and to be honest; they were doing not much better than me but acted like absolute divas, had a problem and negative opinion about everything without ever offering a solution.

I may have been somewhat wayward but still wanted to come up with something funny and quality too. I had fire in my belly and wanted to strive, it was just the fire was of an erratic nature from time to time.

I chose to work by myself. I turned up one day in a state, someone asked if I was ready for the stand-up comedy assessment to which I said, "The what now?" To be fair, one guy seeing I was in no way prepared said, "Why don't you tell that story I heard you tell the other day in the pub about how you died twice?" I was damned if I could think of anything else so that's what I did.

I've always felt comfortable onstage, could hide in performance. I'd always had people in stitches with my escapades, I didn't think there'd be a way to combine these things. Before long I had everyone in fits of laughter, I couldn't believe it, I entered to indifference and left to rapturous applause.

What I was talking about was housed in tough times but as I'd turned it into something funny it became really cathartic for me even though people were essentially laughing at my pain. I'm surprised I learnt this so early on as it's definitely the path I need to stay on, where my best work will always come from. Often comedians hit a bit of a stumbling block when they don't do this.

Comedy's the one thing where it's a blessing to have been through hardship because you've got things to talk about and it's that that makes you stand out and about time to get something positive from all the shite.

People now seemed to be willing to give me the time of day. The head of drama came up to me and said, "Whatever it was I had it" and she was another that said this whilst smoking a cigar and twiddling her moustache. I felt special, something shifted, I'd never felt like anything was my calling before and I'm not in any way saying I was the finished project, I still don't think I am, I just felt like it was something I was supposed to do, something I could get really good at.

With acting I was great in Cornwall but the auditions then moving away made me realise I was just a big fish in a small pond there, out of that pond I was no more than average. Also with acting on the whole you're being other people and reading other people's stuff whereas with comedy it's more on you, writing what you're going to say is an extra layer of creativity, plus you don't have to rely on as many other people too.

I don't think the head of drama knew what she was letting herself in for, she quickly became a sort of West Midlands mother figure, I wouldn't have made it through the course if it wasn't for her.

Batty was off with Tiger but that was ok as I'd made some great friends on campus, but because I'd met them whilst drunk I'd convinced myself that the personality they got on with was entirely down to alcohol so that was the level I needed to maintain at all times.

I only went to six lessons in my first year, the head of drama told me I was an alcoholic so took me to a doctor to confirm this in the form of a doctors note to get extenuated circumstances in order to pass the first year.

I was bombarding her with all sorts of nonsense, emailing her with dramas at 3am. As is the way with a lot of people that have been abused, I was searching for validation from men. I wanted to be loved but was attracting the wrong people because I was an absolute piss-can so only fuck boys were ever interested but I didn't understand any of that because destructive sex was all I knew. And that was what I was bothering the poor head of drama with at 3am.

24.) One of the girls

My new friends were 'girly girls,' I wasn't used to going to places where there were dress codes. I wanted to have the same experiences everyone else had so would adhere to dress codes with help from my new pals. I ended up having a quite drastic image revamp, I think I lost a bit of who I was.

I started wearing dresses and that but one thing I wouldn't budge on were heels (I walk like a farmer at the best of times, never mind when my feet are higher than they're supposed to be) so I wore little pump things. In this new attire I couldn't believe the difference in how people were speaking to me, especially men. Even though it was all very shallow and I knew that, I must also admit it was still good for the ego as I'd always been the friend of the beautiful ones but now apparently beautiful was I.

I thought everyone would come from far and wide to experience living away from home like me but the amount of people that even though they lived on campus had parents just down the road was astounding. Even Batty went home quite a bit, I wasn't ready yet.

'Irish' was the only person that seemed to be on campus as much as I was. Everyone called her Irish because she was from Ireland. People really are shit aren't they.

I'm not sure we'd have been friends had we not been thrown together as she cared about having her nails done, hair extensions, things like that and I'd rather be poked in the fanny by a squid. I unintentionally fell into a friendship with someone that thought it was a good thing to go out with a footballer, she also got me watching 'The Kardashians' and I will never forgive her for that.

There were many wonderful things about Irish though, one was her loyalty - I'll always love her for that. The first weekend everyone went home to their parents I saw as a good time to get my clothes washed but embarrassingly I didn't know how to use a washing machine. Irish did so passed on her knowledge and it was then we became very good chums.

Irish lived with an older girl called Leanna who introduced herself as, 'Lej,' a nickname she gave herself. Short for Legend, not window ledge. I liked her though, although now I'm not sure why, perhaps because she'd constantly tell you how great she was so I bought in to her hype? She dazzled in confidence I could only dream of.

If things weren't done her way or she wasn't spoken to or included in things exactly how she wanted to be though: she'd not only be upset - She'd not tell you why she was upset but tell everyone else and exclude you from everything you'd usually be involved in.

We always had the TV on back home, I didn't realise how much I appreciated the background noise until I moved away without one, I just didn't think I'd need one. I'd come back from lessons, no-one else would be about, I'd sit on the edge of my bed in my eerily quiet room and It'd really hit home how far away from my mum I was.

I'd get letters from my mum and auntie so would spend quite a bit of time at reception chatting to the security guards as that's where you had to go to collect post. I mentioned missing a television in passing and they said an international student had left one last year so there was one going spare if I wanted it. I couldn't believe how kind they were, Batty and I started to chat to them all the time, they started to feel like family. They even give me a card with money sellotaped in it for my birthday.

25.) Be still my beating heart

Everything changed when I met Dwayne. We were out one night at The Student Union and there was this 6ft 9 guy that literally stood out from the crowd. This particular day I'd had a mixing bowl of gin jelly for tea, all washed down with two litres of White Star cider (this was all whilst getting ready, to go out to drink). He was dancing away in a fitted brown striped polo shirt, I said to Batty, "Oh my gosh, look at him, he's so good looking," she told me to go and talk to him. Until she said that I didn't even think that'd be an option as I assumed someone so handsome wouldn't want anything to do with me. Off I went. I remember chatting, dancing and laughing with him and then off we went back to mine and had a magnificent time. It was definitely the first time I'd enjoyed sex.

Afterwards he fell asleep, was snoring like an absolute growler and all my friends were still out so I was like, "Fuck this" so put my clothes back on, rang a taxi and off I went to whichever name the club had changed to now for tax avoidance purposes. I drank three shots of Goldschläger on arrival, sicked up blood in the toilets, was squawking about that to anyone that would listen, friends happened to be in the cubicles, "Is that Dyer we hear?" It was like we hadn't seen each other for years, we danced lots, drank more and had a very splendid time.

We then went back to halls, carried on drinking until the sun came up, I finally got back to my room, got back into bed, went to sleep and he was none the wiser.

When we woke up I was so ill, went to the bathroom to be sick but because it was an ensuite he could hear everything. I wasn't too fussed though because I assumed I wouldn't see him again so was really surprised when he text later that day asking if I wanted to go out with him sometime. I could not believe my luck! The problem was I had no experience in dating someone I actually really fancied so was more than happy to listen to everyone else because they'd had more experience. Leanna said, "When someone messages be sure to wait at least 12 hours before you reply." I think someone had told him something similar because it'd take us 24 hours to establish a mutual, "Hello" "How's it going?"

I've always hated speaking on the phone, I get really anxious about it, I think it's the urgency of it, that whoever it is needs to speak to you right now at that particular moment. I also find it difficult to hear what people are saying and so many people mumble so find it far easier to make out what's being said if I have their mouth to watch.

If someone says they'll ring me that call then seems to send my whole day into looming dread. I can't do anything or relax knowing that the call is coming - I know that sounds a bit much but that's how it is for me. Anyway, Dwayne was a phone call kind of guy. I'd often panic then let it ring out which he took as I didn't answer because I was "up to no good" when that just wasn't how it was.

It's annoying when people are like that because they like speaking on the phone. Just because YOU like speaking on the phone doesn't mean the person that doesn't is wrong, they just don't like a thing that you do.

We were two people that didn't know each other. When we tried we'd butt heads, he didn't get me or my sense of humour and also would take offence to things that in no way were worth getting offended about.

"I've always felt it a shame my mum ended up a cleaner as she's such a talented artist so it would've been great for her to follow that passion"

"It pisses me off when people say stuff like that…"

Oh fuck off. What would piss you off about wanting better for people? Also I wasn't saying there's anything wrong with being a cleaner. We were never singing from the same hymn sheet, I was just blinded by how much I fancied him.

He would never honour timings and plans; we'd arrange a time to meet, he'd be hours late because he'd be watching a basketball match in the sports hall and upon explaining he'd fail to see why this was a dick move. He even could've asked me to go with him.

There was always an excuse and when he would grace me with his presence he was so tired so would just want sex and then fall asleep. I know that's how we started but he was the one that pushed to be more than that with his "I can see us together for ever" and, "I'm really falling for you."

One morning I woke up and everything was wet, I asked him what it was and he said, "Sorry babe, I dreamt you were a urinal." He'd dreamed I was a urinal and pissed up my back. He'd pissed the bed and blamed me for giving him cider. He didn't even help clean it up, he rushed off muttering how he'd be back later which of course he wasn't. I was that weirdo at 4am putting their mattress on the balcony to air for the whole of halls to see.

Even in this blinded by beauty state I realised I deserved more, I told him this so he said he'd make an effort. He came out one night, I was in the toilets for a while because a friend had not long found out her mum had cancer so was really upset, I was obviously comforting her, I came back to him grinding up against some girl to which he blamed on me because I was gone for ages.

26.) A new fish in town

A new girl moved in to halls, Raquel, we quickly became friends. She started seeing another friend of mine, "Big Barry" I thought she was a character, sassy, knew who she was, really fun but my other friends weren't keen and didn't trust her, looking back there were definite signs of strange behaviour.

Barry and I were close as I used to drink with him and the boys that lived in his block. We first met in the laundrette, I'd come to collect my lovely dry washing from the dryer to find some absolute tit had taken it out of the dryer and had put it back in the washing machine then turned it on for another wash. I was livid, asked Barry who did it, he said, "Jane Doe" but I didn't know that's the name given when someone's unknown so I was walking around campus shouting and screaming asking anyone I saw if their name was "Jane Doe" to try and get justice for my washing.

I've always got so worked up about the smallest of issues, perhaps it's some sort of coping mechanism to distract myself from the bigger worries, of which I sort of disconnect myself from.

Mine and Barry's relationship became strained because Raquel would tell me she didn't want to be left alone with him. After what I'd been through I obviously would never want anyone to be in a situation that could lead to things someone wasn't 100% comfortable with so when she invited me to spend time with them I'd always come. Unbeknown to me she was telling Barry she wanted to be alone with him and had no idea why I kept turning up to interrupt them!

I opened up to her about my past and told her how there was something about Dwayne I didn't trust to which she said, "All that's in your head to do with your childhood and your mental health" I spoke to him and he said, "All that's in your head to do with your childhood and your mental health."

Of course they were getting together behind my back. Barry let Leanna and I in Raquel's block to confront her and all she could say was, "All that's in your head to do with your childhood and your mental health…" That's when I snapped, don't gaslight me. OWN YOUR SHIT.

Out of my peripheral vision this thing passed me. It was my fist and it was about to punch her in the head. I'm not a fighter though, misjudged it entirely, went for the forehead and broke my hand.

Raquel didn't see herself as having done anything wrong, got a friend to hit her around the head with a tin of beans so she had an even bigger lump on her head then went to the police. The following day I got up, was in the kitchen eating my Cheerio's when the police came and took me away in my zebra print winceyette pyjamas. Once at the police station they put me in a cell with a guy with one tooth. He told me he invented toothpaste,

"I'm not sure you did Steve"
"Well, if you think about it - If someone with lots of teeth invented it wouldn't it be called teethpaste?"

I couldn't argue with that logic.

Despite putting me in a cell, one policeman was actually quite pleasant, "How on earth has this happened? You're clearly better than this, stop fighting over boys" he said and he was right.

27.) Fishy aftermath

I regretted punching Raquel because the moment I did I made her the victim. Of course it became gossip around campus, people that didn't know me thought I was some sort of thug which was ridiculous and because it happened on campus and the police were informed I had to have meetings about my fists of fury to see if I was about to be kicked out.

I was devastated, there was no way I could go back to Cornwall and prove that idiot in the TK Maxx cash office right. In order to stay I had to write a grovelling letter of apology to Raquel. The guy in charge guided me in the sort of thing to say but when he spelt her name it didn't seem right but he insisted it was and you just trust these people in important positions, that they know best.

"Dear Raccal…"

Leanna was with me when I punched Raquel, she was on coke and couldn't have egged me on any more than if she had eggs on her person and as mentioned Barry let us in so they both played their part.

Barry was devastated about it all as he loved her and even though she denied it to everyone they definitely had some sort of relationship. He now wasn't speaking to me and fuck knows what he said to Leanna because she was now doing her weird thing where she'd cut you out without telling you why. I really needed someone then too as it was a nightmare at dinnertime cutting up food with a broken hand. Thank goodness for Irish.

Barry and I never spoke again which was shame. He chose an exposed liar over his friend.

28.) Minding my own business

A lot of friendships I've had have suffered because I've gotten too involved in who they're dating: perhaps I'll never change there actually because I'm not going to just stand by if someone I love is not being treated how they should be. Projecting much Harriet?

As last reported Tiger enrolled in a course and new life in a city he had no desire to be on / in, it was just another way he could control lovely Batty.

As we know, university life is big on the drinking. Tiger could not handle his drink, he was a vile drunk, horrid to so many people, the only reason no-one punched him in the forehead was because everyone loved Batty. Once he was dressed up as "Army" (as you do at uni) he was drunk and angry at Batty for some pathetic reason as she never actually ever did anything wrong; and he lobbed this big toy gun behind him in the Student Union and it hit a security guard on the head. She was furious but nothing was done because of Batty.

He spat in Batty's face twice on two different nights out that I knew of. He spat in mine once too, I couldn't believe that someone would be that disrespectful to the person he claimed to love and her friend. I chased him and tried to throw a bin at him. I'd rather someone took a swing for me than spat in my face, absolutely vile.

I'd say to Batty, "How can you be with someone that does that not only to you but your friends too?" and she'd just whine,

"I hate being in the middle."
"This is definitely not being in the middle, the middle is between what is right and what is wrong and you're choosing the side of what is wrong."

The next instance of his exemplary behaviour was him accusing her of cheating, checking her bins for condoms etc when it of course turned out that it was actually him that had been snogging a girl they both had to see every day in their dance class.

One evening Tiger came bursting into my room in just his boxers, covered in blood, totally panicked. He was shouting that we needed to get to the hospital. They'd been having kinky times, he'd blindfolded Batty, she'd got disorientated and fallen through a mirror, he led me to her then passed out.

There was blood everywhere and glass sticking out of mainly her arms, legs, and arse so I instructed her to, "Elevate everything!" I then went to the fridge to grab my beers and off we went to hospital.

We were there for ages, Batty had to have stitches.

We ended up there again not long after because he was chasing her, she ran in to a windowsill and part of it broke off and went in her hand.

All this was another reason I thought he was no good for her, this type of shit should not be happening. A worrying part of the windowsill episode was we thought the doctor had taken it all out but a few months later Batty got chatting to a girl on a night out who was doing a nursing degree who looked shocked when shown Batty's hand, she oddly had tweezers on her and picked out another chunk of windowsill that was still in there.

29.) Sorry dad

We had a marvellous end of uni ball, all got dressed up lovely. For some reason even though they weren't leaving for another year Raquel and her friends came to our leavers ball. That was her all over, she once formed some sort of gang and hosted the 'initiation?' on my birthday hoping people would come to that instead, it was all very immature and tiresome. Of course she'd brought Dwayne too, just for that extra little jab in the gut.

There was an awards ceremony at the ball and one of the awards was for 'Funniest Person' as voted by everyone and I won it. I was really chuffed but hadn't banked on it happening so didn't know what to say, I looked out and saw Raquel and co, I panicked and garbled out, "I'd like to thank my dad for having really funny sperm" which still makes me cringe.

I took the award, got off stage and this guy from my classes in Wolverhampton asked if he could have a look at the award, he picked it up to look at it then dropped it, it smashed everywhere and I heard a lone voice say, "Now that's funny". I laughed hysterically to show I didn't care but I was embarrassed.

I wasn't drunk enough for this social whatever it was and was dressed like I was going to the races, not my vibe at all. What even is 'a fascinator?'

After that we had a lovely dinner, was sat around a table with good eggs, and Tiger. The drinks flowed, the night did a total 360 and ended up being wonderfully splendid. We had fancy photos taken too then flipped our heels (the one time I wore heels) off and danced long in to the night.

30.) Let loose in the real world

Everyone was gutted to be leaving uni because they were going back home to live whereas Batty, Irish and I were moving in with each other so couldn't wait.

We lived in a house that when we went to first view was a building site and to be honest not a massive amount had changed for when we moved in. There was always a problem, the estate agents would send their friend round to fix everything but their friend would just come and slag them off, telling us all the corners they'd cut.

Once we were eating dinner in the dining room when a liquid entity exploded all over our food, we looked up and there was a massive fungus growing on the ceiling that had suddenly burst and their handy man friend took great glee in telling us, "That's because there's a hole in the bath upstairs and instead of replacing it they'd just taped over it so the water's seeping through and around."

Direct debits can't have been as common then because we'd have to go to the office at the end of every month to pay the rent and it'd be full of people complaining but they couldn't have cared less.

I desperately needed a job; during the holidays whilst at uni I was still working at the TK Maxx back home. The holiday before I'd be leaving for good there was a new manager that walked around like he was the Fonz. He told everyone he used to go out with Natalie Imbruglia and Michelle Collins but one day Michelle actually came in to the store and didn't have the foggiest idea who he was so I do believe he was talking nonsense.

Every so often the staff would go out drinking after work. One time the Fonz and I got hammered, ended up having a smooch and he was absolutely mortified with himself.

Weeks later I asked him if I could transfer to the Birmingham store for good. "Yes, of course" he said and immediately went to sort it out, all was sorted for me to start full-time the moment uni finished which was perfect.

That day I turned up in full uniform to be told no-one had sorted anything out for me. Also because I worked at the one back home for so long they used to let me do my own name badges so not only was I stood there in uniform for a job that never existed: I was also wearing a name badge that said, 'Queen Latifah.'

I ended up getting a different job in retail at the local shopping centre. It was a bit deflating that after finishing a three year degree I was pretty much where I was before but such is life. I lasted one day at a different shop in the same complex but it was just awful but good looking people. I bent over to pick the Hoover up and two guys came either side and pretending to hump me. I put down the Hoover, walked off in to the night and never did I return.

I had an interview for another place and instantly knew it was more for me. There were so many different characters, most people that worked there had other things than just the shop - They were in bands / were DJs, wanted to get into fashion etc which was exactly what I needed, to be around creative people. When I handed my CV in I was greeted by the security guard Dick, he seemed charming and couldn't do enough to help. He called down a little friendly guy called Barnaby that bounced down the stairs and seemed lovely too.

By this point I was going out with a guy called Wally. He was my first boyfriend since the Dwayne debacle, he seemed more honest but another one that didn't get my sense of humour.

I of course am the common denominator in these cases though so perhaps it is my sense of humour that's the problem. He worked at Boots in London which I loved because that's what mum did when she first left home, she worked at the one in High Street Kensington and would serve celebrities - I loved hearing her stories about them. She said Joanna Lumley would always look a bit grubby and never wear a bra. Probably because she just popped out for some Alka-Seltzer and hadn't banked on getting judged by you Vivian!

It was a long distance relationship but I quite enjoyed the commute to London every other weekend. Probably because we weren't compatible I became anxious around him and wasn't able to eat properly, I knew deep down we were on different pages, I think I just didn't want another failed relationship and always invested too much in people that weren't suitable. We were together for about six months, I thought we were in love, he came up to visit me as normal, we were having a nice time when suddenly he said,

"I'm going into the army"
"Really? Oh right, this is the first I've heard about it, when?"
"I leave on Wednesday."

I was crushed as he was going to be in the parachute regiment which was apparently really intense so he didn't know when or if he'd be able to speak to me for months at a time and he didn't understand that I was well within my rights to be a bit pissed off about it because it was the first I'd been told, with three days notice. I joked, "You'll do anything to get away from me won't you?" to which he got so angry and couldn't believe that, "I was being like that."

Off he went, he'd arrange to ring but never would when he said which wasn't enough for someone that needed a bit of assurance.

I got chlamydia, was beside myself about it, hadn't cheated on Wally so must've got it from someone before. Dwayne and I always wore a condom, but is it true that that doesn't make a difference with chlamydia?

Obviously I couldn't casually ring Wally to talk about it so ended up texting him telling him. Weeks went by and I was in a state, I wasn't eating, my life was dictated by the anxiety of not knowing what was happening. Weeks later he finally got back in touch, "I don't know why you're letting it bother you so much, it might've been me that gave it to you."

I think that clearly shows how I held myself in such low regard that it didn't even cross my mind that it wouldn't have been me at fault.

He made a big thing about having some time off before I went home to Cornwall for Christmas, he wanted to "treat me how I should be treated" and "start making it up to me." I thought this was a lovely gesture. We decided on a "little Christmas" (Christmas before Christmas) so I cooked a fantastic roast dinner, all his presents were wrapped underneath a Christmas tree and I was there waiting for him in my Christmas hat. He never showed up and didn't think to let me know.

31.) An unexpected trip to Cornwall

Graduation day was approaching. My wonderful mum was at the hairdressers when she started to have a stroke in the middle of having her hair cut. The hairdresser exclaimed, "I think we need to ring an ambulance" to which she barked, "You can finish cutting my bloody hair first!"

As I wasn't in Cornwall no-one 'wanted to worry me' so my dad and Joe majorly underplayed it. I had a feeling something wasn't right so rang the hospital and spoke to mum, she sounded like she'd strawpedoed a magnum of gin, slurringly awful bless her, I came home on the first train I could. The price that last minute train ticket cost was unforgivable: if you're reading this Mr Branson, you should be ashamed of yourself!

It was the first time I'd ever seen Joe pleased to see me, the house was an absolute mess and there amongst it tending to a burnt out saucepan was him. I came through the door and his face lit up - They really should've been honest with me from the off.

I'm not sure mum was ever the same after the stroke, although knowing how much some people are affected after I think she was quite lucky as she could still speak, didn't need a wheel chair, could still get around. Psychologically it probably affected her most, her confidence was shot and she became nervous leaving the house. The left side of her body suffered too, as it often does, unlucky for her she was left handed and said left hand became a bit gnarled, all bent up like a pigeon foot.

She tried so hard to get better for graduation but was just not up to it. She was really missed but of course we all understood.

I ended up getting a 2:1 which was a Christmas miracle! I also got given an award for comedy and general turnaround which was nice. I had a really nice time with dad and Joe, they stayed at Brindley Place in Birmingham which was fancy, we ate delicious food and it was so nice to have them there.

We actually ended up almost missing graduation due to becoming enthralled by a Jeremy Kyle episode about that very angry religious family in America that hate all "the gays."

Mum of course had to have lots of time off work to which the people she worked with weren't happy about as they didn't think she needed it. They obviously didn't know her like they thought they did as mum didn't have a chancing bone in her body. Other than WHEN SHE HAD A STROKE she'd had no days off sick, not one.

She got in her head too much which we all know can be the downside of spending too much time with yourself. She became quite cantankerous, neurotic and bossy, something she usually wasn't. I told her to stop it, she did and said sorry and Joe said thank you.

I think stress helped cause the stroke, she'd had years of it with dad and then a neighbour of hers, Sandy behaved like an absolute turd. Mum and Sandy were friends for years. Mum would get two free tickets per week to the cinema (a perk for cleaning it) so would often take her.

Every house where we lived had a garage, above the row of garages were big cliffs, the cliffs were crumbly and little bits would always come down but one day it got really bad and loads came down and went through peoples garages. One garage had a whole families Christmas presents in it that were squashed. Measures had to be put into place to secure the rest of the cliffs so it didn't happen again.

The houses for a lot of folk that lived there were holiday homes so money was not an issue, they just paid the thousand odd pounds there and then needed to keep the cliffs up. Mum and her next door neighbour Hamish were the only two that didn't. Sandy was on the housing committee and decided that mum and Hamish weren't paying for the sole reason that they were being awkward, not because they didn't have any money. She turned against them, became nasty and threatening, it really hurt mum and really took its toll on her wellbeing. She didn't have the money so didn't know what to do.

Sandy had a creepy little husband that once left a note on Gordon's sisters windscreen calling her a slag because she'd parked in the wrong place. They were a mean spirited pair of creatures.

In the end Sandy ended up sorting the cliff out no bother, not sure why this couldn't be done from the start.

Mum was so forgiving, she didn't want the negativity. Straight after all this Sandy was hovering around our garden as she'd noticed a slate we had in it and asked if she could have it for her roof. Cheeky bitch! Mum should've smashed it over her head but instead she was only too happy to give it to her because that's the sort of person she was.

Despite ceiling explosions living with Batty and Irish was great until Tiger started coming round more and more. It became clear that Batty would be moving on and away with him which was sad as it felt like bad had prevailed. Batty departed and slid back in to exactly the same life she had before she left for uni, same job, back living with her parents, same everything. Batty said her and Tiger didn't argue when they moved back to Cornwall but that's because no-one was calling him out on his behaviour anymore, he does exactly what he wants with no repercussions.

They got married, Irish and I didn't go to the wedding, I think we were only invited to the reception. Batty was upset with us because we didn't go to the hen do. It's a tricky one because some would argue that whatever makes a friend happy should make you happy but my thinking was that someone so special should be treated in no other way. She could never see it from my point of view and I could never see it from hers. There's definitely no hard feelings or anything like that but there's not that closeness any more, the last couple of times I saw her it just wasn't the same, she was different, she'd lost the shine of loveliness she always had around her.

This may come across a harsh and I guess it isn't specifically just about her, I've known it with a few people - If you spend 24 hours a day / seven days a week with a cunt, eventually you're going to end up bit of a cunt.

Sorry if you don't like that word as I know a lot of people don't. I say it a couple of times in this book when I believe it's called for, although admittedly I did take out loads. Through doing comedy I'm desensitised by it because I hear it so often. I see it as only a word really, if you hate it that much may I suggest moving to Barnsley? I did a gig there once and whilst I was onstage a man in the audience squared up to me twice which definitely warranted me calling him a cunt and the whole audience turned against me saying, "Women shouldn't say that word."

32.) Fungus House

Remember the, 'Patch up the bath' estate agents? When we were moving out we asked them if there was anything else we needed to do, did we need to put the fact we were leaving in writing? They said no but when it was time to move they charged us an extra month rent saying we didn't tell them. When we had the final walk around they were trying to charge us for a million things that were already an issue when we arrived. I was angered by how much they were trying to take advantage and ended up hurtling my Happy Days clock at one of the guys, it skimmed his ear. He looked at me like I was generally terrifying, ran out of the house, got in to his car, drove off and that was that.

I was so depressed. Dick the security guard at work had infiltrated someone I could rely on and as always my ability of picking good men had well and truly departed, well had never arrived to be honest, I might as well have picked them via Tombola.

He asked me out and we went to a trendy place in Birmingham, the music was shite, he loved funky house which to me sounded plinky plunky, I couldn't work out how I was supposed to dance to it. The date was ok, perhaps his true self was seeping out because I started to find him a bit selfish. He wasn't asking me anything, it was all about him and what he wanted, he was also one of them that goes on about how any girl he gets with has to have amazing banter to "match his" when his is barely tickling the soles of his feet, let alone anywhere else. Like with Leanna though, because he kept telling me how great he was I thought, "Ah so the feelings in my gut must be incorrect because if anyone knows him it'd be him!"

He made this big thing saying how drunk I was so said he had to come back to mine to make sure I was ok when I didn't feel drunk at all. He wouldn't leave so I slept with him because that's what he wanted. He had a shower then left and was off with me the day after.

I didn't want any awkwardness at work so asked to meet up on his day off to talk about whatever his problem now was. We went for ice-cream, I'd never found the idea of rum and raisin appealing before but threw caution to the wind and was most pleasantly surprised. Speaking of wind it was a very windy day, we went outside with our ice-creams and sat in deckchairs, the top of my ice-cream blew off and landed on my chest and he laughed which broke the ice… cream?

He started to be really nice, we ended up sleeping together again (I know) but after he said, "You need to stop doing this to me as I have a girlfriend." You fucking what pal?

Every day this young girl used to come into the store and he said it was his sister but it turned out it was his daughter, who the fuck lies about having a daughter? Then I found out he found an Anne Summers bag that a customer had left in the shop, he tracked down the woman then fucked her with the dildo that was in the bag in the women's toilets. Quite the imagery that is, sorry.

He also told me he was 34 but was definitely older and definitely a compulsive liar. I asked around and one girl that'd been working there for years told me, "I did think it strange that we celebrated his 32nd birthday at least twice." He was 50.

33.) New reality. TV

I was at such a cross-roads in my life, didn't have a clue what to do, felt hopeless, was in need of another change. People had always said I'd be good on the TV programme, Big Brother, I didn't know what I thought about that but a guy I worked with said he was going to audition and did I want to come? That year was supposed to be the last one ever so I thought, "Fuck it!"

I saw it for what it was straight away so knew how to play it. My friend got knocked out in the first round, he was a really confident guy but for some reason he just crumbled when he had to say three facts about himself. I said 1.) My dad left my mum after 30 years of marriage for another man 2.) I died twice when I was 17 and 3.) I once ate 14 pasties in one sitting. Number three was the only lie but bizarrely the least far fetched one.

I sailed through. I then had to fill out a form and talk to a panel of absolute arseholes. I'm not sure if they were actors, producers or who they were but one thing I did know was, one woman in particular was rude. She told me I was a failure at everything and that's why I was there. I knew she was after a rise so remained calm, told her she was wrong, "I've still so much time to achieve what I want but you not so much."

I was told to wait outside, I was pretty sure it was the end of the line when this lovely lady came up to me and said, "You're through to the next round, would you please come back tomorrow?"

It almost took me until tomorrow to leave the building as it was all held in a science museum and I got lost in the planetarium trying to find the exit. In the end security had to guide me out through the tannoy, because of all the stars and sky it felt like god was talking to me. Perhaps it was a sign?

I came back the next day so pumped, it was great to have a bit of secret excitement. I filled out some more forms and got put in a sort of focus group with other hopefuls which was in a circle with newspapers in the middle, we were told to talk about current affairs. They clearly wanted us to argue, the people I was put with were vacuous and desperate, I hoped it didn't make me the same for being there. These people would literally sell their souls whereas I just wanted a break from the mundane.

I could tell in the discussions that some people didn't even mean what they were saying, everything was them second guessing what they thought, 'Big Brother' would want to hear. I become introverted in situations like that so just sat back and listened, piping up only when these idiots said anything so ridiculous I couldn't let it slide. There was a girl I recognised from the shopping centre I worked in, she looked like if the Cadbury's caramel rabbit was a human, very beautiful, no chat though. The world was once again safe from implosion.

Then I had to chat to a man in a box like it was a diary room. He knew everything about me. I started to get irritated, "How do you know so much about me?" Forgetting I'd put it all in a form.

So yes, I had my little weekend full of all that and then returned to work on Monday, I felt a bit smug as I wasn't allowed to tell anyone what had happened. Time went by without hearing about it so thought, "Well it was a bit of excitement whilst it lasted" but then they rang me at work to tell me I was still very much in the game, next stop was London where I'd have to wait in a coffee shop until a girl with a pink umbrella walked past and I was to follow. It was all so cloak and dagger, I loved it!

Thank goodness it was sunny or else I could've followed a lot of people with a pink umbrella. There was another girl from the coffee shop that also followed her so we bonded over that. Then we were all led to a room and shot.

Joking.

Coffee gal and I both smoked so would excitedly natter during cigarette breaks. We had to do all these eating tasks (which admittedly was more 'I'm a Celebrity Get Me Out of Here,' 'Bush-tucker Trial' style). I remember looking at one guy retching eating pickled herring and another eating cat food thinking, "What is this?"

At the end of the day everyone had to vote who they'd get rid of out of the group. My coffee shop cigarette buddy with picked me, she said I was her competition. JUDAS!

One guy said me because my hair, "Was shit like his mums" which was much fairer: I had a proper a mum bob on the go.

There were a few more of these days, days of running through absolute hoops. Another time I was to meet someone outside a different cafe, I was waiting there for so long that when someone did appear I was so surprised that I shot forwards without looking what was in front of me and got snapped up in a sandwich-board.

The paper work they required was far more than anyone ever has readily available. I got a phone call one evening from someone who was most irate with me because I'd just guessed the address of my doctors.

"You've absolutely blown your chance here."
"It's season ten, no-one gives a fuck any more, calm down!"

Then in another curveball they rang me up again with "Right you're in the trial house, pack a big enough suitcase that you could go straight into the main house after if need be."

The trial house is the actual house but before they start filming properly, it's to see if it's all liveable, to test out the tasks and to basically watch the people they're still on the fence about.

I was told to head to London Marylebone Station and when I get there "There'll be a car with a sign that says, 'Mrs Peabody' in the window, get in and the driver will take you to the hotel you're staying at in Elstree." Once there someone came to my room to take my food order, they said I could have anything I wanted and I thought that was the best thing ever. I had chicken and chips.

On the morning I was going into the house I was held up in a room with a minder, they were so nice. We had to go through my stuff and decide what I could and couldn't take with me. Anything too pattern-y had to be taken out because it messed with the cameras and anything with a logo on had to be covered up with black gaffe tape. When they were finally ready for us to go in I got bundled into a golf buggy, a mime mask was used to cover my face and a towel was thrown over my head. Davina McCall presented it at the time but of course she wasn't there as I entered this 'Trial House,' or indeed an audience at all, just the builders who were there working on the house, they all clapped and cheered as I went in.

I was first in and not long after a French guy came in too. I can't remember his name but I do remember that he was incapable of talking to anyone without looking at himself in the mirrors.

There was a girl I quite liked, she reminded me of Nikki Grahame from an earlier Big Brother who I always thought was such a character. This girl made me laugh because she was in a hurry on her way to the house so hurriedly picked up some sandals from a market to wear but in her haste one was a size five and the other was a size seven.

Nothing was natural about it, every conversation was forced. We were in the house but everyone was all too aware that it wasn't the real one so there was this desperation to try and be the person "they were looking for."

I quit smoking before I'd come in but the moment I went in I started again.

Once the house had filled up, we congregated in the smoking area when Big Brother's voice came booming out, "Will the two most popular housemates come to the diary room." Everyone rushed up, then it was decided that there should be a vote, it was decided me and Daz but Cadbury's Bunny of course was there and far more bothered about it than me so was more than welcome to take my place and with that off she and Daz went. They were now the "Chosen ones" and got their suitcases and beds for the night whereas we had to wear spandex, sleep on pallets and eat 'gruel' that tasted like pencil shavings mixed with Doritos.

We'd wake up so hungry having hardly slept as the chosen ones breezed on by with a McDonalds breakfast. Then shit got interesting. We were told that under no uncertain terms were we allowed to ever step foot in their bedroom, that was only for the chosen ones, not the pallet partakers.

Luke was one of those people that would argue for the sake of arguing, he was definitely trying to play the game and definitely not one to try and keep the peace. In the middle of the afternoon he just ran in and out of the chosen ones bedroom 'for a laugh.' Nothing was said about it and I distinctly remember someone saying, "Perhaps Big Brother didn't see it" which made me laugh.

We were all eating dinner that night when suddenly a screen above our heads turned on and there was a guy that looked like Beaker from The Muppets sitting in the diary room and Big Brother was saying that at this certain time the rules were broken and as a punishment Beaker was to live in the house for 24 hours then decide who he'd replace out of the two 'Chosen ones.'

It turned out Beaker knew Daz from karate tournaments in the real world so Bunny got the heave ho. I felt a bit bad for her because she'd cut her Mauritian honeymoon short for this, but then she was beautiful with lots of money and people that loved her so was sure she'd be fine. The only person I really got on with was a guy from Bradford. He was a bit of a diva but funny with it, I felt he was more self aware than everyone gave him credit for, his life long dream was to be on Big Brother.

Everyone other than Bradford, Beaker, Daz and I were teenagers, it was like living in 'freshers week' 24/7. Bradford was hot headed and got in to an argument with the younger ones, (over what I can't even remember) everyone was arguing, I didn't know what was happening or what had been said. Bradford then kicked off at me because I didn't hug him after the argument which puzzled me. He then smashed through the fire exit and off he went.

I felt shit he felt I wasn't there for him, although I don't think, "Being there for someone" is reliant on whether or not you hug a person after a day or so of meeting them. I had a little cry whilst gathering his belongings. It was sad he'd let other people dictate his time in there when it had meant so much to him, although perhaps that was part of his plan, I didn't know.

There was a task for everyone to win their suitcases back. They said they needed the two most agile people so they picked me and this kid Jimmy. We had these lycra suits (Big Brother must've got a very good deal on bulk lycra) we were in a pitch black room, we were at one end and had to get to the other but there were loads of light beam lasers that we weren't allowed to touch but could only be seen when we sprayed this mist (just water in a spray bottle) on them. We worked really well together and because everything was so amplified in there, we hadn't slept properly for days now, it was far beyond any normal amount of time to be in spandex so were desperate to win everyone their stuff back and the intensity to do so was immense. We did and we were heroes, everyone was throwing us in the air and marching around with us on their shoulders it was great!

I wondered if the same "health checks" were done for me as they were for everyone as the psychiatrist that assessed me just threw a packet of cigarettes at a wall and shouted, "That's your privacy" and that was about it. Beaker that replaced Bunny was definitely not in a good place, this was clear to see. His brother had not long died of a drug overdose and he thought one of us had stolen his only photo of him. He was shouting, screaming, trying to fight everyone but it was in the bottom of his bag. He needed time to grieve bless him.

I like to think I'm quite a loosey goosey person but when living with people I definitely expect a certain level of respect as that's what I give, it's rude not to. No-one seemed to be mindful of anyone else in this house, I woke up at about 4am once to find a guy I called Foxy Bingo because he looked like the fox from a TV bingo advert banging saucepans to wake everyone up, making sheep noises and writing his name in ketchup on the walls. What the fuck was I a part of?

It was the 10th anniversary of Big Brother so there were various activities to celebrate this. There was a quiz about all the previous seasons, we won and I was called to the diary room to get the prize which was some wine and lager. As I was coming out the French guy that entered the house after me tried to snatch the wine out of my hand.

Me: "What are you doing?"
Him: "I'm French so of course the wine is mine"
Me: ………. ? ………..
Him: Give it here!
Me: "Shut the fuck up Pepe Le Pew."

"Jesus Harriet, what have you just said?" seemed to be the general consensus of the other housemates. I spent the rest of the time worrying I was going to be kicked out for a racist slur, even thought I personally felt he'd behaved like an absolute dick and I'd just called him out on it in a very witty and under appreciated way.

I wasn't keen on Daz at first as he was very flirty but had the name of a girl tattooed on his forearm who I'm sure at the beginning he said she was his girlfriend but as time went on he said was his ex. He had a leathery face, injected himself with tanning injections and was yeah, most things I don't understand in a person. He started to pay me a lot of attention and was very complementary so I guess he started to wear me down a bit. He asked if I'd get in his bed for snuggles, I would not. He said he was going to turn up to where I worked on my lunch break just to spend that hour with me which I thought was nice. There was still a niggle of none trust but he also seemed like a gentleman that could treat me nice so when we left and I knew him and I were both being dropped off to the same station (we each had a car with a driver to take us, we weren't allowed to travel together even though we were going to the same place) I waited at the drop off point so I could chat to him away from cameras and everyone but he never came. I've been since told he confided in someone else saying he was only showing interest in me because he thought I was guaranteed to be chosen for the main house.

The girl that reminded me of Nicky Grahame was apparently a sneaky beaker too as she was a law graduate and knew only full well that her shoes were different sizes, she thought it'd be amusing. It was.

34.) Back to old reality

Mum said, "It'll be a blessing if you get in and a blessing if you don't." She was right. I didn't get in but I made peace with that quickly. I was grateful for the experience of it all but was happy to have it under the radar.

Work had become toxic and not only when it came to Dick. I got on well with the boss, Elsa she was having a tough time too but nevertheless we'd always have a laugh. She was "seeing" Barnaby that also worked there, he was desperately trying to work his way up the company. When I say she was seeing him - She was in love with him and he was fucking her when no-one else was. He was so bubbly until you knew him. He said to her once, "I don't want to be with you, I want to be with someone I'm proud to walk down the street with" which was appalling.

They were fucking at work and generally bringing all their shit to work too. So many young pretty girls would hand their CV's in wanting to get weekend work, Barnaby would flirt with them in front of Elsa, she'd get upset then take it out on everyone else and be stomping around in a mood and unnecessarily barking at everyone for the rest of the day.

The final straw for me was when a young, sweet girl started, it was her first job and how Elsa was speaking to her was humiliating, she was shouting and belittling her in front of customers for no reason so I told Elsa she was wrong. She was livid so banished me to go and clean the toilets like I was Cinderella then took me out to fire escape to shout at me, she told me I was acting like a child and I told her she was acting like a nobhead and for that I was given a warning.

This is an insight in to my state of mind then. I thought, "I can't be here anymore but it's coming up to Christmas and I still want to get paid so the only thing for it is – I'm going to have to break my arm with a mallet."

I went to Poundland, bought a mallet (I told someone this once and they interjected with, "No, that didn't happen, you can't get a mallet in Poundland" to which I replied, "Out of all of this, that's what you've got a problem with?") I did get a mallet from Poundland. At the time I lived with Irish.

"Hello Irish, can you please break my arm with this mallet?"
"Hello Harriet, you don't have to ask me twice"

With that she started hitting me on the arm with this mallet. After a while nothing was really happening so I said, "You're going to have to stop now, you're just tenderising me."

I brought her into the hall-way pointed at a table there and said, "Right, what we'll have to do now is, I'll put my arm on this table then you run up, jump on it, arm will snap, job's a good 'un."

She was half a mile down the road taking a run up, she came bounding in, I've got my arm on the table, she goes to jump, I lose my nerve and move my arm out the way at the last second and she human cannonballs on to the concrete floor. I said, "Right, stop your nonsense, what you'll have to do now is set your alarm for a sporadic time in the night, don't tell me when and just burst in my bedroom, swinging at my head with the mallet." She's crying because she's cracked her knee-caps. She got time off work, I did not.

It was then we decided I needed to hand in my resignation regardless. It was time go to and see a doctor too, I'd become unbearable to live with.

The doctor was disinterested, he wouldn't look at me and asked me a list of questions from a sheet of paper which I found to be circumstantial, things like, "Do you have a high sex drive?" which I felt was ridiculous because when I'm with someone I'm at it like the clappers but when I'm not I don't give it much thought. He could have quite easily got the answers needed by talking to me like a human.

From his questions he came to the conclusion I had bipolar and prescribed a plethora of medication. I rang mum to run it by her, "Oh Harriet, don't be taking any of that, you're just eccentric." So I didn't.

35.) Giving comedy a proper go

I needed to be creative, even Elsa had known that and would make up none existent job titles for me like, 'Denim Specialist.' I desperately wanted to be a comedian, that was what I needed to focus on now.

I didn't know what 'a circuit' was so if there were gigs to do, I didn't understand how to get them. I Googled, 'Comedy gigs' and a page for a company that books gigs all over the country popped up. I emailed them and got a reply asking for my bio? This was short for biography right? So I sent back well, practically this book, *"I was born in Cornwall" "My dad left my mum for another man"* and so on and so forth. I didn't know by bio they meant what I'd been doing thus far comedy wise. How would I know unless I knew, ya know?

Strangely they gave me a gig regardless and goodness it was a shift from anything I'd done at uni. Again, I was a big fish in such a minuscule pond, by the end of it I was known as some sort of comedy genius whereas obviously in the actual world that most definitely was not the case.

The women I'd seen on TV doing stand-up were people like Rhona Cameron so that's what I thought I was supposed to look like so I mustered a cheap black polyester suit from goodness knows where. My drinking was still an issue so when I arrived at the gig and they said there was a free bar for the acts I absolutely hammered it. The room was a little basement, really funky, almost cave-like with a cabaret set-up, tables with tablecloths and Jack Daniel's bottles with candles stuck in them on top.

Six pints of snake-bite in I've stumbled in to one of these tables, everything's fallen over and a candle's ended up setting the tablecloth alight. As chance would have it there happened to be a fire-person in the room who put it out. The gig went as you can imagine, I didn't really have any jokes, I told that long and waffling probably more than ten minute story about how I died twice. Everyone in the audience looked confused, although one member did come up to me after the gig saying he couldn't quite believe that was my first gig out of uni but he was either being very kind, wanted to sleep with me or was simply in awe that my polyester suit hadn't gone up in flames.

I continued to drink until 3am when they stopped serving, looked out of the window and saw a man fingering a woman but his technique was to swing his arm back and fourth, easy mistake to make though as I've often mistook fingering for bowling.

That was the last night that gig offered a free bar to the acts.

I really wanted to learn and get better but as far as I could make out there wasn't much of a comedy scene in Birmingham so I put on a night at a pub in Digbeth.

Some friends had ordered food there once but it never came, turned out the chef had dropped dead whilst cooking it.

A guy from uni ran a comedy course for kids to try make to money when leaving uni so roped me in to help. Neither of us were equipped to do this but arrogance and naivety overrode at the time.

One kid stood out, he did a routine that was brilliant but I've since realised it wasn't even his, it was Rod Gilbert's luggage routine, he even had the bloody suitcase handle!

I put on my own gig on to 'hone my craft,' I asked him to open the night then I put an ad on Starnow to find someone to compere / host it and I closed it. The guy I got to compere was awful, at one point he started singing Luther Vandross.

I gathered people from my uni days and despite Luther it went brilliantly, I was ecstatic. It was these little moments that kept me going and let me know that there was something else for me other than existing in jobs I didn't enjoy.

I started to do them regularly, I'd compere them but would break up bits I'd written into sections, there'd be no chatting to the audience / crowd work or anything like that and if I did ever do a set I'd have written a brand new one each time which was about 20 minutes of absolute shite, I didn't have a clue. I needed to just work on a solid five minutes, building up to ten, etc.

Even though these nights were often disastrous and poorly attended they served a purpose as introduced me to people that were on the circuit and knew how it all worked.

I soon had a few nights, in equally unsuitable venues. I made the mistake of asking comedians what they charged instead of just offering a fee and realised the moment I saw them onstage that they were open spots trying their luck. An open spot is a new act that isn't ready for paid work yet so gigs as much as possible on bills with people that are doing it full-time to see how it's done, I guess a bit like an apprenticeship really. It separates the wheat from the chaff because the ones it's not for fall at this hurdle as it takes a special kind of nutter / comedian to traipse all over the country at stupid hours of the day for no money.

One chancer had definitely watched Russel Kane a lot. He had the same blond streak quaffed into the front of his hair that Russell had at the time, same skinny jeans and was thrusting and lunging around all over the shop. You get that a lot in comedy, a lot of new acts that have grown up loving or now love whoever's flavour of the month and often without even realising they become an amalgamation of them.

There were a lot Frankie Boyle wannabe's at this time too. I saw a guy open once with a shock bit about "fucking babies," I was horrified, there's no time or place for that, and that's not what Frankie Boyle does. There were quite a few Nick Helm wannabe's too, always Stewart Lee's, folk that wanted to be like Sarah Millican and most recently James Acaster. Comedy is such a saturated field, I can categorically say you won't get anywhere if you're just a less good version of someone else.

36.) The Teacher

I got a job teaching drama at a drama and dance academy in Birmingham and it was perfect for pursuing comedy as was essentially just a Saturday job but I was making as much as I previously was getting for working a full-time week in retail.

Business wise what the owner (Nicky) had built up at this academy was astounding. It was in an area of Birmingham that was quite deprived (pretty sure she got funding because of that) and hundreds of kids would turn up hungry for mainly dance but also drama and singing too. With now a degree in Drama and Theatre, that's what I did, taught the drama side of it.

The first thing to strike me was how Nicky spoke to the kids, it was awful: shouting, screaming and grabbing them and dragging them in to place if they weren't doing something right.

The students, parents, other teachers - Everyone was united in disliking Nicky but most definitely from a safe distance, behind her back.

The parents were martyrs, they knew it was wrong, were constantly whinging about it, had been whinging about it long before I arrived but still put their kids through it and even themselves as they volunteered to help there so nothing would change.

They put on shows every year and competed in competitions too, when I arrived so many kids were disheartened because the same ones always got lead parts in everything. She always had the kids she deemed to be "the best looking" at the forefront and the others all snarled and squished up at the back. I was there to change that much to her confusion.

I did private acting classes and pride myself on the fact every kid I taught in those lessons got into the drama school of their choice.

Nicky's family all helped out too. Her mum had one eye and the kids used to call her Mike (from Monsters Inc) she was neurotic and would shuffle about urgently but never seemed to actually get anywhere. Nicky would scream at her in front of everyone and she'd then shuffle off urgently to nowhere once again.

Nicky had a little boy that she sadly lost to cot death and despite what they all said behind her back it was touching how everyone rallied around and were there for her during that awful time. I really felt for her, I'm not sure it's ever possible to get over something like that.

The only person I quite liked was the woman that worked on the tuck shop, she seemed on my level, the one thing that threw me was her job outside the academy was a bailiff which didn't fit the person I thought she was.

I started to open up to her and she to me. Her daughter had a kid really young, the father was a nightmare and once when the kid was playing in the garden jumped over the fence with a machete to try and take him. I said if they ever needed to get away from it all they could come stay at mine as it was a machete free zone.

Mentally of course I still wasn't in a good place, still wasn't getting help for the mental illness I clearly had. I'd get the bus every Saturday morning and on said bus without fail there'd always be the same teenagers fighting and setting fire to things. I'd arrive to a patronising and condescending morning meeting from Nicky to set us up for the day as we meant to go on and then a kid would come running in saying they'd lost a shoe and Nicky would scream at them, make them feel worthless and by now it'd only be 8:00am.

I confided in the tuck shop lady that I didn't want to be there, from what she told me she felt the same. Outside of work we'd text and for a reason I'm still unsure of she forwarded Nicky my texts saying I wanted to leave. Who does that? A chuffing bailiff, that's who!

Nicky was pregnant again by this point and told me that if I left the stress of having to find a replacement would most likely cause her to have a miscarriage. Is everywhere like this or do I just have remarkable skills to be able to always seek out toxic workplaces?

37.) The Doctor and the comedian

Online dating used to have a real stigma attached but now it's probably the main place people meet. Every time some sort of relationship would finish with someone I'd have to wait at least a year or so before dabbling in the next because usually I'd be too emotionally spent to even entertain another.

I met a guy online called Englebert, he was a doctor. I wanted a nice guy and he seemed that, although a doctor going out with a comedian is like, well a doctor going out with a comedian.

We got on well at first (although my gut did tell me he wasn't right for me on the first date but as usual I just ignored it). I couldn't eat when around him again, I got myself really worked up that he was going to finish with me and this paranoia was eventually most likely the cause of the end.

I don't think I've ever met anyone as posh as his friends, we all went for dinner and one saddled straight up to us the moment we arrived and guffawed, "Englebert guess what I just did? I took the new Audi TT for a test drive," He made some sort of "Fnaw, fnaw" sound and off he went. I'd say that summed up the group as a whole. They were obviously intelligent and successful but I've never known such inane vacuous drivel. Nothing fun about any of them, they were all so corporate which was another thing that put me on edge.

I couldn't eat a thing and they all assumed that I was someone that was always on a diet, "Yes, this diet's one I've been working on for a while now, it's called the crippling anxiety diet."

We went for dinner another time (YOU CAN SEE I'M HAVING DIFFICULTY, PLEASE STOP INSISTING WE GO OUT TO DINNER) and I opened up about choosing not to drink anymore because of how much I used to. He was so judgemental, his whole demeanour changed, I felt I could be myself even less.

My past is very much a part of me so the quicker it's accepted, the quicker we can move on. Plus I didn't even give him the meat of it all, more of an Amuse-bouche.

We started to not even talk to each other. He'd gotten in some trouble at work he wasn't opening up to me about and I was becoming more mentally ill by the second, it was shit.

Before we met I recorded an episode of Dinner Date (the dating version of Come Dine Wine Me) it was funny, a laugh, it still gets repeated ten years later because it's the only one where someone almost died. I didn't cook my chicken properly so as a result my date was pissing out of his bum after eating it.

It was finally aired when I was with Englebert on my birthday. He turned up late, was in a foul mood, I showed him the episode as I thought and still think it was funny, he didn't laugh once.

We went to Nando's, he was terrible company. Some students at the next table recognised me from the episode, we were all laughing, joking and chatting away and Englebert walked off in a huff. And that was the end of that.

He turned up at a comedy night a few years later. He didn't get the hint that I'd been hiding in a toilet for 20 minutes to avoid him. He accosted me when I came out and said, "I've seen you've got an agent and you're doing really well." He was shallow and very 'keeping up appearances,' he had to have a flash car and live a flash lifestyle, I didn't fit into that and didn't want to. That's all him and a lot of guys want, not a girlfriend like they think they do but someone just there to look good, blend / be moulded in to their life and PLEASE no unique personality traits or out of the box career choice.

I was gutted when it didn't work out, not because I would miss him though, more because it was another failed attempt at finding someone. I was relieved financially because I didn't want him to feel like I

was with him because he had money so I'd insist on
paying for everything which sent me into financial
despair.

38.) Sun, sea and what now?

Irish and I were going through break-ups at similar times so decided to take a holiday. I'd never been on a holiday that wasn't with school / college or with my parents trying to fix a marriage before and definitely hadn't booked one. Irish seemed to know what she was doing so I was more than happy to let her sort it out, I transferred my half over from the beloved overdraft.

She chose the destination holiday, Magaluf. I didn't know anything about Magaluf, I genuinely thought we'd be sightseeing and taking in the culture, oh we'd be sightseeing all right!

I had no idea about Magaluf's reputation, although did think it strange that whenever I told anyone I was going there they'd pull the same face and say, "Shagaluf?"

We arrived at the hotel at 10am and were given shots by these club reps that must've been on commission for signing people up to activities because from the moment we arrived they were trying to guilt trip us in to doing them. "No Gibbo your booze cruise does not sound appealing, the only thing I can think of worse than being in this room with you would be to be stuck on a tiny boat with you."

Throughout the duration of the holiday every time I ordered a pint as if by magic Gibbo would appear and shout in my ear, "Down it, down it, down it" It was already wearing thin and we were only 30 minutes in to the holiday.

Magaluf is someone's with anxiety's worse nightmare, I'd look around and dislike everyone, all anyone was doing was shouting, drinking, shouting about drinking, fucking and shouting about fucking!

I'm not sure I even knew was anxiety was then, let alone knew I suffered with it. I think Irish thought I was just being difficult and I assumed that's what it was too.

I didn't realise that people deal with breakups differently. Like I've said, I go on a man ban, I don't want anything to do with anyone, whereas Irish was more, "I'm going to grab all the dick and I'm going to grab it right now."

On the first night she went off with a guy and I was left not knowing anyone abroad. They went back to our apartment and must've been very vigorous in what they were doing because when I returned there was dust everywhere. The room was sparse so I'm not sure where it had dislodged from? Perhaps from someones loins?

Irish left me with the friend of the guy she'd gone off with who now expected me to get with him because my friend had gone off with his. These days I'd just say, "I don't want to do that" but I used to worry about hurting a morons feelings so I oddly gave him a fake phone number and went, "Ring me, let's sort a date" to try get rid of him not banking on him ringing the number straight away, he did and obviously my phone didn't ring so he started shouting at me in the middle of the club.

All this was occurring at a popcorn party so I walked away from him, took my shoe's off, filled them with popcorn and went to a toilet cubicle to sit down and eat. I love toilet cubicles, they section you off from all the nonsense, if ever you can't find me in life, just head to the nearest toilet and there I shall be.

Irish finally came back and I was so pleased to see her but also livid. She seemed very sorry though so all was forgiven, after all we were on holiday. The next day we were walking through the main strip and everyone was shouting out to me, "Oi dancing girl" apparently I was having dance-offs with everyone and was now Magaluf queen of freestyle dance so it seemed I'd actually had a far better time than I thought I had.

We shouldn't have gone on holiday with each other, Magaluf was not for me and Irish just wanted to be annihilated 24/7 but I at this point was trying to get off that ride. Also both of us suffer with the most horrific hangovers so on the nights we'd get like that we'd be being physically sick until 9pm the next day. It's absolutely madness anyone would want to drink when they know they'd be that ill all the next day, although that's another thing we initially bonded over.

The DJ in our hotel was originally from Newquay so we were trying to work out if we knew each other as everyone knows everyone in Cornwall. Irish got peculiar about it because she said she blatantly fancied me. Just because someone's gay doesn't mean they fancy me plus so what if she did? Irish made an issue out of nothing so then it felt like "a thing" whenever I spoke to her when it's just nice especially when you're away to chat to people from home as it's automatically one massive thing you've got in common without even knowing each other yet.

There was one guy Irish got with that was nice but had a superman tattoo that covered most of his torso. He was from Sheffield and he ended up at ours for longer than expected because when he went back to his room there was some sort of drama, I'm pretty sure his door slammed shut locking him out but when it slammed shut he'd trapped his towel in it so he came back to us naked and very embarrassed. The next day we were sunbathing and along he came with a bunch of flowers and a box of chocolates for Irish which was really sweet. She thanked him by throwing up in the pool.

One night we were out, I was wearing a little dress and a guy on the dance floor tried to put his finger up my arse. I went mad and tried to knock the shit out of him. I was quite shaken up, found Irish, told her what had happened and she said, "What do you expect, you're in Magaluf?"

Another day it was raining so we were indoors at the hotel bar having a few beers when Gibbo came running in, picked me up and threw me into the pool with all my clothes on. I was furious, went to our room to get changed, the rain had by then stopped so I hung my clothes up on the balcony then went back downstairs to carry on drinking, I'm chatting away when suddenly Irish exclaims, "Umm Harriet" so I've followed her gaze to see all my clothes have blown off the balcony and in to the trees: knickers and all, what a nightmare.

I found the pool guy with the very large stick to help me get it all down but he didn't know any English and I didn't know any Spanish, neither of us knew what the other was saying but after a lot of pointing and charade like gestures I believed I had communicated successfully what I was after and off he went. Later that day I went back to my room to find him lying on my bed wearing all my clothes.

As we were leaving the moronic club rep that pushed me in the pool was bent over tying his shoe laces up so I pushed him in,

"But I can't swim"
"That's all right Gibbo, just down it, down it, down it!"

Irish and I will always be friends but it was a little strained after that holiday. I guess all the partying and drinking that we initially bonded over had long before stopped being fun for me.

39.) Carry On house sharing

A big reason Irish had stayed around after uni was because of her boyfriend so once that had dissolved and once she'd had a rambunctious holiday to let some steam off she decided to move back to Ireland.

I moved closer to Birmingham City centre. The flat was fantastic, really modern, the only problem was I was moving in with a stranger I'd met via Spareroom.com. She had the sense of humour of someone out of a Carry On Film and other than being overtly sexual she really didn't have a personality.

On her birthday I figured I should make an effort though so hung out with her and her friends. Together were like a boxset of all the Carry On films.

She had a boyfriend who I always thought was ok (if a bit of a posh boy) but he'd completely switch after having a drink and on this occasion suddenly called her a slut because she twanged an elastic band in his general direction and it hit him in the head. He threw his drink everywhere and stormed off. Despite this they were actually well suited.

On days where she knew I had early starts she wouldn't even mention to me that she was having all these friends round taking over the entire flat other than my room (which was something I guess) and being loud as fuck all night so I wouldn't get any sleep. I even heard one of her friends say once when they were still up at 6am having not gone to sleep yet whilst I was getting ready for work, "Ssssshhh we're going to wake Harriet up" and she said, "I really don't give a fuck."

My mum came to visit (of which I gave more than sufficient notice) and her boyfriend was there just wondering around in his boxers. That's not on is it? Or were we being too sensitive? Just put some trousers on mate, me mum's round, plus you don't even live here.

Some people just aren't for you are they and they were that. I guess that's the risk though isn't it when finding people on those sites because you don't know who they are, they could be anyone, even dangerous so in that respect I'd "lucked out."

40.) New act hustle

I was now doing bits of paid comedy work so was gigging as often as I could. To be honest there weren't lots of comedians I enjoyed watching. There was one guy Gavin who I'd seen compere previously and it was like nothing I'd ever seen before, he was so quick, was definitely inspired by Def Comedy Jam comedians and whenever he was on the audience didn't care about anyone else that was on, they just wanted him onstage all night.

He regularly hosted a new act night which was renowned in the Northwest, the audience get to vote the acts off by holding up a card if they don't like you because comedy's always at its best when it's turned into sport. The first couple of times I did it I was struggling to find my voice onstage. I was confused because each time I gigged some male comedian or another would come up to me after and tell me what I needed to do different and foolishly I'd take it onboard for the next gig each and every time.

The second time I did the night I did a full set of one liner jokes which failed miserable and I was carded off within a minute or so. Gavin came onstage after and said, "It should've worked but it didn't" and for some reason that gave me hope. I messaged him on Facebook after, saying it was nice to meet him and asked if he had any advice. He said, "Don't give up because you're something different in a sea of beige" which was also just what I needed.

Then I was hustling like a mutha, oh boy I hustled and if I wasn't gigging I'd go on Facebook, look at comedy events happening then cold email / message the person whose night it was asking if they could fit in an extra open spot or if they'd bear me in mind if someone dropped out. Believe it or not at that time it actually worked.

I also did another of those new act sport type shows, this one in particular was brutal. One of the acts had a ferret puppet that was part of her act, she struggled then as she was coming offstage a woman in the audience told her she was shit and punched her. A massive fight broke out, there were hair extensions everywhere. The compere had to call the break early. I was on after, was stiff with terror and had convinced myself I could no longer speak. It actually went fine, I think it was just ferret based humour they had a problem with that night.

I'll never understand how something someone does onstage can be not to your taste that much that you think, "Well, there's only one thing for it - Immediate violence."

I did it a few more times as although not nice to do it was simple enough to get a gig there and is such an iconic space. The last time I did it as I was leaving the stage the compere Alex Boardman whispered in my ear, "You shouldn't be doing these anymore, message me on Facebook." I of course did and he turned out to be one of the most supportive people in comedy. He instantly sent a blanket email to all his contacts asking them to give me a spot on their bill.

The Comedy Store London got back pretty much straight away,

"There's a spot this weekend on the late show if you fancy it?"
"Yes, wow, that's amazing."

I had a pal who was really into comedy so we went down together on the train, had a whole night of it and stayed over. I'd only really seen the new act nights at these venues so to see comedy ran at this level, it was amazing, life changing even.

I was on with Kevin Bridges, he was so good and so lovely. I was nervously chatting away to everyone backstage and after I'd been on Kevin said that I was funnier offstage than onstage and needed to be more me. He was right, that was what I knew from the start but along the way I'd somehow allowed myself to be moulded by other peoples nonsense.

As a result of Kevin's wiseness I did something some said was stupid - I had a tryout spot at another big club the following week but I scrapped the whole set

I was using as it was shit, bits I'd picked up from other people, not comics, friends / family shit jokes and opinions that weren't mine.

None of it was really me which was silly because I'd had a whole life of experiences to talk about. I scrapped the set, wrote a new one, gigged every night with the new one to try and shape it in to something decent. The gig was ok (definitely not great but not awful) but I was one step closer to being the act I wanted to be.

41.) New love

Eventually I progressed to a Thursday at the new act night in the Northwest. The spot on Thursday was the one you'd do before doing full weekends which is what the professional acts do. I was still living in Birmingham so got the coach up. Gavin was compering again, once again he was brilliant, my spot went well too, he and I got on well, he gave me a lift to the coach station after the gig. I messaged him after thanking him and from then we started chatting regularly.

After weeks of solid chatting he rang me, "Right, I'm coming to Birmingham to hang out" We'd both already made it clear by now that we liked each other so I guess this was our first date? We went to various Birmingham drinking spots and had cocktails, I couldn't be arsed to get in to my drinking issues so just drank with him which I don't think was the best idea. We got on well enough, I kissed him, he took the piss because we were smoking at the time so it wasn't very romantic. I was more worried because when we kissed I didn't feel anything but thought I'd somehow got what I was feeling wrong? Always listen to initial gut feelings.

I told him I didn't want to get into a relationship because they always end in disaster, he assured me that we'd always be friends now so if anything happened he'd be honest with me to avoid anything ending in disaster.

Sex was odd, I'm not sure I ever fancied him but he acted like it was an honour and privilege to be with him so I yet again assumed it couldn't possibly be me that was right so figured it had to be down to what had happened in my past so opened up to him about it which he was actually really nice about, said all the right things which was the turning point, I now started to like him a whole lot more.

He was gigging abroad and left me a voicemail in the early hours one morning telling me he loved me and that was it I was now in with bells on. Ring-a-ding.

Sadly though his words never matched his actions, other than that one time he was quite judgemental, always in performance mode and had an opinion about everything I did. "I'm not doing the dishes wrong Gavin. Are they clean, yes? Then wind your bloody neck in."

The anxious not able to eat when in a relationship problem was at its worst. Food was now feeling stuck in my throat so I'd start retching. It felt impossible to swallow unless washing it down with water.

As it was something he didn't do and didn't understand he was dismissive and impatient. Even the things I was able to wash down with water that had been easier to keep down like fruit etc were now rising up and I started to be sick after every meal. I told him about this, he was "grossed out," so I was now doing it in secret so as not to bother him.

He still always insisted on going for food which of course was making it worse. On occasion he'd ask where I wanted to eat so I'd come up with tapas type places where it's small amounts of food that might be easier to pick at and stomach but that's not what he wanted so he'd still end up picking what he wanted. The next time he'd ask I'd say, "It's up to you" as he'd pick regardless. He'd say, "It really puts me off a woman when they can't make a decision, I can't stand indecisive women."

The most I ever ate and kept down when I was with him was when we went for dinner for me to meet a friend of his. His friend was lovely, we got on really well to which he sulked after, "I'm used to being the funny one in a relationship."

People I knew worked at the club he regularly performed at and started to sort of congratulate me which I didn't understand. Turned out he'd started doing material about how good at sucking dick I was but would say, "It's so good it makes you wonder where on earth she's been" which was degrading and not a compliment at all.

Despite the anguish we'd chat every day, regularly and consistently, then one evening that changed. He was at a wedding so was to be expected that correspondence would be sparser but even then something didn't feel right and when he did get back in touch a day or so later he was distant.

I had a feeling that something had happened. Someone told me later about a comedian he used to sleep with being at the wedding that told him she had no knickers on, they both disappeared together and weren't seen for the rest of the night.

He could never just tell the truth even though from the beginning that was what he promised, he was given a "get out" right at the start but instead ground me down until I loved him.

Instead of breaking up with me he decided the best thing to do was ignore me until I went away. On a quest for closure I kept ringing him until he finally answered to tell him that I knew he didn't want to be with me anymore, to which he finally agreed. I mean what even is that?

Unbeknown to me by this point he was getting with another comedian on the circuit and everyone knew but me until at least a year later someone mentioned it whilst we were car-sharing which was humiliating. People I knew looked up to him like I once did so didn't tell me, just left me to it.

42.) Fucking Manchester

I had a gig outside of Manchester and was supposed to be staying at Gavin's after but obviously that was no longer happening.

I was doing a lot of gigs for one promoter in particular at the time, he was a fan of what I was doing but it went a bit downhill after this gig. I was on in the middle because that's where the newer acts go, I'm quirky and high energy which was working when I was on after a lower energy act because it was a nice contrast but at this gig for the first time I was on after an even higher energy act so what I did sort of jarred and I didn't have the skills yet to reset it.

Perhaps I was a bit off too, although sometimes when feeling low I find I bring a different kind of energy that more often than not will do really well. Perhaps it's when caring goes out the window as your mind's on other stuff, although I'm not sure of the logic behind that because if you always didn't care surely that wouldn't work either?

Anyway, I struggled at the gig so felt even worse after, then I missed the train I needed to get in order to make the coach in Manchester that'd take me back to Birmingham. I thought, "Fuck it" and bought two glasses of wine and sat down to watch the rest of the show until I could catch another train back into Manchester where I'd figure out what I was going to do from there. I was glad I stayed, Paul McCaffrey closing it was one of the funniest things I'd ever seen. It might have been one of those 'had to of been there' moments but I'll try to explain nevertheless: He was doing his set as usual when a guy came bursting through the doors shouting, "Is Sandra in here?" everyone was like, "Who the fuck is Sandra?" He made his apologies then left. About three minutes later another door flung open, a lady was standing there so Paul said, "Are you Sandra?" She was! Everyone was laughing and Paul sent her the other way after him but then he suddenly appeared at the other door that Sandra had just been at and this happened so many times with Paul so wonderfully narrating the whole thing, it was so good to laugh away at something so delightfully silly.

I got on the next train to Manchester feeling a little better after wine and laughter but was worried about where I was going to stay as public transport options had long since passed. I had these people I knew in Manchester but they were better friends with Gavin so felt it wasn't an option to get in touch with them.

"I'll find a hotel in Manchester, how hard can that be?"

Of course it happened to be the day Manchester United was playing Manchester City so everywhere was absolutely rammed, no room at the inn anywhere. My phone battery by now was also dying plus this was when internet on phones wasn't as good and I didn't know my way around Manchester at all. Everyone was so drunk, loud and stumbling about so I decided to pretend I was in a computer game having to avoid zombies, I put my headphones on, my soundtrack to this would be Bonnie Tyler's 'Holding Out for a Hero' which actually helped for a bit. Then I walked past a nightclub where there was a group of women outside smoking, they must've seen me manoeuvring zombies whilst mouthing along to Bonnie because they started shouting that I was a weirdo then threw their lit cigarettes at my face. I didn't feel like playing my game anymore.

By this point it was about 2am, I'd been to almost every hotel in Manchester, I crossed a road because Google maps was saying there's a Jurors Inn up ahead, at the same time, a stag do's approaching. Upon seeing me they looked at each other, got their nobs out and started to chase me. It was horrible, they were laughing hysterically with their dicks out. I was so tired, their faces looked demonic, the good thing though was through cowering I could now see The Jurors Inn up ahead.

I ran straight in there and asked the receptionist if there were any rooms left, he said one and I could've kissed him. I burst out crying, he said, "Are you ok?" to which I replied, "The willies were chasing me." He didn't know how to reply to that.

The room was £200 which I was gutted about because I was struggling with money so my mum gave me £200 the day before to help so this meant all that would be gone. I couldn't go back out there though so handed him my card with a very sad look on my face and up I went to my very pricy room. That is pricy isn't it? Is that what a lot of people spend on one room for one night? Feels ludicrous to me.

I opened the door to the room and there's three beds in it, I'd never felt so lonely in all my life. I made sure I set my alarm at various times so got to sleep in each one.

43.) Top boy bants

The people I knew in Manchester became good friends. I felt I was perhaps ready to leave Birmingham, the comedians seemed a bit more driven in Manchester.

In Birmingham it was pretty much my pal Flint and I, one guy even said to us that he couldn't be as close with us anymore because we wanted to make a career out of comedy so were too serious about it all. Why would anyone spend so much time on something they didn't want to get the most out of?

We're working class, doing jobs we don't enjoy, here's an option to change that, why would that ever be a bad thing?

There was a group of us that used to car-share to gigs together, all lads and me. I can take 'banter' as much as the next person but it became toxic. The harshness of said banter would be dictated by whatever was going on in that persons life and the main instigator was Zain. He was miserable, his dad committed suicide when he was a kid, he lived with his mum but they weren't getting along, he was definitely the best comedian out of us all but would self sabotage whenever an opportunity came up. I could relate to a certain degree but it was still frustrating, it got to the point where nothing positive would ever come out of his mouth.

I wasn't in the best place at the time with my default setting of constantly feeling suicidal so being all squashed up in a car for hours with all this negativity was not helping. After a gig "The person that did the shittest needs to sit in the back, what you doing sitting in the front? You should be in the boot!" HA HA HA HA HA HA. Comedy's the only thing I find solace in at the moment, please don't take that too.

We were friends though so he'd ring and we'd chat, I'd tell him it would get me down, he'd say he'd go easier, I'd say I'd try to be less sensitive but then it'd just go straight back to how it was.

Then I got a gig, the guy wanted me to sort the whole line-up, I asked Zain to open for £100. The whole line-up was in a group message, in which I said we all were to do our best stuff as we mainly did new stuff / unpaid or very low paid stuff together and I felt pressure because the guy had trusted me to book the entire night with some people he hadn't seen. Zain was angry, said I thought I was better than him and was speaking to him like an idiot, like he should be grateful to me. "Oh wind your neck in, that's not what it was at all" He refused to do the gig.

By this point I'd been signed by an agent and top banter Zain had already left me a voicemail telling me he hoped they'd drop me soon so I'd have to go back to teaching, I know in his head it was a joke but it was the straw that broke my camels back. I'd had enough: friends should lift each other up not constantly chip away and knock each other down.

I tried talking to him before and it didn't work so whether right or wrong I blocked him on everything and cut him out. We didn't speak for years but were due to be at the Edinburgh Fringe festival one year and had the same friends, I didn't want it to be awkward so messaged him saying well, what I just said but he messaged back, "Who's this?"

A year or so after we were on the same gig together, I tried to be civil but he wasn't having any of it, it turned out he was really hurt as considered us to be such good mates which I felt really bad about but he wasn't seeing it from another point of view. We were both doing the trial spot at this gig so were to a certain degree trying to impress the bookers and I don't think, "Having a domestic" was what they had in mind.

"Can we please get on because we're gigging together?"
"No, you cut me out"
"But you were a massive dick"
"But you cut me out…"

This ensued for a while.

I had a friend with me too that was stood there mouthing, "What is happening?"

He's all bluster so apologised by message later but there was no way his pride was going to let him do that in front of anyone. We've now been friends again for a while and he still brings it up, he's even brought it up when we've both been at a gig together and he's been onstage, twice.

To be fair to him, he's a completely different person now, he's happy. I think him previously was a perfect example of the phrase, "Misery loves company."

He had some savings he said he was going to use to start a new life for himself in London to finally make 'a proper go of comedy.' He'd been saying that for so many years though that we thought it was empty words by this point and he was never going to make the leap. He finally did and it all turned out splendidly, he was at a shit gig one day with hardly anyone in but an agent, they signed him, he worked hard and all these wonderful things started happening for him.

With London prices though he couldn't live there and just do comedy so also worked as a doorman.

He kept on with the hard work, got his big break and got to perform on Live at The Apollo which was especially great because only a couple of months prior to this he was working as security in the exact same building which is really inspiring.

44.) Moving to fucking Manchester

The agent I got was based in Manchester, they used to have an act on their books who also lived in Birmingham who told me she wished she'd moved to Manchester when she was with them as she felt it would have opened up more opportunities. I saw her as the ghost of Christmas future, was already feeling a bit stifled in Birmingham so thought it was time to make the move.

I didn't make the best first impression joining this agency as I didn't know figs were diarrhetic and ate three tins of the bastard things and couldn't stop shitting so had to cancel the first gig I had down to do for them.

A lot of newer comedians do this, I was no different - It was flattering to have someone enjoy what I do enough to have me on their books. A pal Beatrice worked for them too, I definitely trusted her and what she thought too. Taking her out of the equation though, looking back they as an agency said all the right things but I don't think they did much more than I could do myself. The biggest problem would be instead of admitting they couldn't do some things, they'd pretend they could so a lot of things would take forever to never materialise.

When moving to Manchester I made the monumental mistake of not finding a flat until the last minute, it was a nightmare viewing flats because I was moving cities and didn't drive. There's only so much you can see from a photo too and as a result I ended up staying in a dome of doom.

I moved in with this couple Krissy and Donny and the moment I met them and saw the flat in person I felt like crying. It wasn't filthy or anything like that, it and them were just very cold, I also felt the amount of rent I was paying was far too much for what it was.

On the first night I went out, got lost on the way home and the battery on my phone was dying so I couldn't use even Google-maps. After a lot of walking around in circles and crying I eventually found my way but then I couldn't get the key they'd given me to fit in the door properly.

Once I finally got in the flat and to my room nothing about it ever felt homely, just empty, lonely, cold and sad. I thought, "I don't know why I was trying to get back so urgently."

If you as a couple are not in a comfortable, safe and stable relationship, there's no way you should be opening your home for someone else to be joining you.

I took pity on Donny at first because although he wasn't the brightest lamb in the kofta she constantly spoke to him like shit. They didn't seem to like each other, I think he especially was just there because it was convenient as she owned the house.

He was obsessed with Manchester United and banned from the city centre whenever there was a home match on because of the trouble he'd previously caused. So yes, I was now living with a football hooligan. Perfect.

The moment the ban got lifted he dumped Krissy in the middle of the street and she took his keys and told him he was not welcome back to the house. I went in the kitchen to get some breakfast and she was there in floods of tears about it all. She went on to tell me he could be really aggressive when he'd had a drink,

"Once he punched a hole in a wall and another time he pissed in your bed."
"Excuse me, what?"

The same day Krissy took his keys she was going away on a course for a few days so told me to make sure he didn't come back and of course I agreed because I'm all about the girl code so off she went and off I went to meet a friend before a gig that night. My friend and I started walking back to my flat for a cup of tea and up ahead I could see the red devil himself waiting outside the front doors to get in.

He wanted to be let in but I had to say, "I'm really sorry, I know this place is more yours than mine but I've been left strict instructions." He was absolutely off his head and sort of pushed his way past, I definitely wasn't going to put my hands on him to try and stop him so text Krissy, "I'm ever so sorry, there wasn't really much I could do without physically stopping him, he made his way in, isn't causing any drama but is a bit worse for wear so I think best to let him sleep it off then I can get him to leave tomorrow?" She replied like what I'd done was unforgivable and told me to get rid of him immediately or he'd get violent. By this point my gig is starting in half an hour or so I don't know what to do. Then Donny's mum's started ringing me because Krissy's told her to get me to get him to hers if that makes sense? This guys own mum is telling me to be careful as, "He has a tendency to get violent."

On this occasion he really was just trying to sleep so I felt so bad having to turf him out, but that's what the gals wanted so that's what had to happen. I got him up, got him to gather his stuff and bundled him in a taxi to his mums. I hotfooted it to the gig and as I was about to step onstage I got a text from the taxi company telling me Donny had left his shoes in the taxi. It was an absolute shit show but at least Krissy was rid of him.

Every day she was away he'd be standing outside looking up at the flat, constantly buzzing and trying to get in. It was the kitchen window he was could see from outside so if I needed to cook I'd sit on the floor, with my arm reaching up to stir my pan so I wouldn't be seen. This was no way to live.

The day she came back I was out gigging so came back late, I went in the kitchen and there was his hat on the side, he was back. I had no problem at all helping her but that needed to be it; as it now was she'd got me to orchestrate her shit to then go back to the way it was the moment she got back. Also how was it going to be anything other than extremely awkward between me and him now?

She told me in such a sheepish manner they'd gotten back together too, she said he was waiting for her on the train platform when she got back in with flowers. Oh he just turned up did he? Just plucked the time of the train you'd be on out of the air? Her parents said about me, "It's a wonder she's still living there with all what happened" which was right. I started to look for a place by myself.

I found a place in a not particularly great part of Manchester but was walking distance to the city centre. The little complex this place was in was actually lovely, it was a tiny one bedroom flat that I instantly fell in love with. It definitely wasn't fancy but could be my own little sanctuary, and I knew I wasn't going to get anything better for the price.

The estate agent and I got on well, in fact he brought some friends to a comedy show of mine a few months later. We had a laugh looking around the flat because there were bongs everywhere, you'd think the current tenants would've moved them out the way when someone was coming round to view the place! He told me when they moved in they needed to see something with the couples previous address on and what the girl gave them was a letter from her doctor telling her she had chlamydia.

I told Krissy and Donny I was moving out, that I wanted to live by myself and they seemed to understand. They said about notice and next months rent and I said, "Right, see if you can find someone first, I don't mind putting an ad out on all the platforms to help."

I moved out then Krissy messaged saying she couldn't find anyone, I've left them in the lurch so could they have the extra months rent. I thought about it and whether right or wrong I said, "No."

I told her to keep what deposit I paid which worked out half a months rent which gave them a bit of extra time to find someone which I thought was fair. I also told her she needed to sort out her relationship before she brings anyone else in to their home because it's not nice to be around, even when they both think it's good.

45.) The Bachelorette Pad

My new next door neighbour was nice but told me the person that lived there before the chlamydia couple hanged himself in the bathroom. I spoke to the estate agent about it who immediately said, "Ah, yes. I didn't know how to tell you."

When you're a comedian (at whatever level) chances are you're offered free drinks most nights which didn't even cross my mind as being a bad thing, it was work after all and "only beer."

If the gig was in Manchester, all the comedians that were on and the stragglers that came to watch the show entirely for the purpose of going out for drinks after would all do exactly that. I'd get home late, pissed and depressed and I'd sit on the toilet thinking I was slurringly chatting to the ghost of the poor chap that had killed himself.

Let me tell you why I thought I was talking to his ghost - I had a lovely friend Sheila that believed in all things paranormal and when she came to visit she said she could feel his presence so asked if he was there and it was then the kitchen light blew! Make of that what you will, I'm just telling you what I saw with my eyes.

A niggle started to arise, frustratingly something about where I was living now wasn't feeling right (other than the ghost). My bins kept looking like someone was going through them then my wall got pulled down one night. I was told it must've been the wind that did it but that didn't sit right with me because not one brick or even a bin or anything else considerably lighter that belonged to anyone else had fallen so how on earth had my whole wall? Finally my emails started to get hacked and I was constantly being locked out of my own account.

One evening my neighbour had some friends round, they were quite loud, I wasn't fussed though so just turned up my TV to drown them out. Hours passed and there was a knock at the door, I'd totally forgotten I had the TV up loud so assumed it'd be about that as his friends had most likely long gone. I opened the door expecting to see him but it's MC, he's somehow found me after all these years. I was in absolute shock, it definitely took me a second or so to register, this was my new life after all, it was very jarring. Whilst stood there trying to compute it all an overwhelming wave of dread and terror washed over me; it wasn't 'to be expected' like it used to be.

I quickly tried to shove him out and shut the door but he just stood there not moving like an absolute boulder. He forced his way in and on me again and all those buried feelings had once again surfaced, I felt pathetic.

He ruined my little isolated sanctuary, my new life, everything was now tarnished. I'd managed to compartmentalise things which I think was how I managed to 'function' by not even associating the things that had happened in Cornwall to me so once I was out of the county a phoenix (of sorts) was allowed to rise from the ashes but now all that had completely been blown apart, the gammy winged phoenix was left scrambling around in the debris.

Sheila kindly took away some furniture I now associated with him as he violently tried to shove a chair leg up me, as oppose to the tender way in which someone would do that.

I quadruple locked myself in with beer, didn't speak to anyone, didn't go to gigs, barely ate, just existed.

Then I got a phone call I was not expecting - MC had hanged himself, I couldn't believe it, Massive Cunt was dead. Such a weight had been lifted, (both metaphorically and physically) I'd resigned myself to the fact I'd never be able to truly relax again but perhaps that could be a possibility now.

Whether it makes me strange or not, something I was now battling with was: MC was still someone that was in my life for such a long time, the closest I'd ever had to a long term relationship: so yes, I hated him with all my being but was it was still a loss of sorts that I was grieving followed by hating myself for entertaining in any way that it was a loss, even one of sorts.

If there was ever a place to go and process all this it was definitely at the worlds biggest arts festival.

46.) An actual shit show

I obviously wasn't thinking straight so was adamant the best thing for me to do would be to now put my focus into my work and go and do my debut hour show at the Edinburgh Fringe Festival.

Some comedians will tell you they come up with their best work under the influence or it doesn't affect their performance but that's wrong and is them trying to justify destructive behaviour they don't want to curb.

The show was called, 'Barking at Aeroplanes' and at the time I thought it was a wonderful show and I was working really hard on it but now I realise it was good but could have been better and I could have worked harder.

I was finding in order to exist without an aching all consuming feeling of pain, sadness and depression my brain had to be fogged but I needed to do it sensibly so was still constantly marinating myself in beer and was now adding a pack of Nytol every day before bed. I know at this point you're thinking, "Jesus Harriet not the Nytol, anything but the Nytol!"

So much time was wasted being drunk or hungover. I wasn't editing the show as much as I needed to be but

I was so in it that I couldn't see it from the outside, I couldn't see it with fresh eyes. I wasn't in the right headspace, body-space, or indeed any space to do it, never mind to do it the best I could. The show was about mental health, about how in my life people had thought I was "mental" when in fact I was just eccentric. Not only was this bullshit, something my mum thought but no-one else did but the more I started to write down my experiences to create material for it the more "just being eccentric" conflicted with how I'd felt since well, for ever. Also all this was a life time worth of issues that I needed to sort through, although it needed to be sorted it wasn't even the time to be thinking about it, I'd not long been assaulted.

I wanted to be alone which is the opposite of what the fringe is. The comedian I was living with had a young family and drove everywhere when back home, didn't have to for a month so wanted to let his hair down. I wanted to be back at our flat but our flat was quite the walk away from where the festival hub was so he'd say, "If you stay for one more drink then I'll walk home with you" then after that drink it'd be "Aw come on dude, just one more" and so on, before I knew it it'd be 7am.

By now with the lack of sleep (even with all the Nytol) hangovers and general indifference to show on top of everything else; the self loathing was through the roof. I wasn't thinking straight (pardon the in advance pun) so didn't turn up to my shows one afternoon and tried to hang myself with my hair straighteners which went horrifically wrong, well I suppose horrifically wrong would be right in this case.

I broke down to Beatrice who was lovely and told me to ring NHS direct who said they weren't too concerned because I "seemed very logical" "Yes, I'm logically going to kill myself!"

They were right though, I'd never be able to put my wonderful mum through it but that meant I was in this limbo where I was forced to exist but didn't want to. They suggested when I get back to Manchester I go to a crisis centre, I did, told a woman there what had been happening and was told, "There's a waiting list but because of what you've been through I'll put you on the emergency one which is eight months." I had a phone call from another nice lady who asked me lots of personal questions; I answered them all as I liked her so asked if I could see her for therapy as I think that's half of it - Finding someone you feel you can be totally honest with, someone you've got a good feeling about. She said what I'd been through was too severe for her to deal with because it sounded like I had extreme PTSD. Over five years later I still haven't heard from anyone else.

Whilst still in Edinburgh my friend Kelly came to stay, I love her dearly but it was not the time for visits, I could barely share a room with myself let alone anyone else. She quite rightly wanted the best experience she could have so wanted to be out and about doing things etc and I felt it was my duty to entertain her. We went to a late night comedy show one night, I was chatting away, put my bag next to me for ten-seconds tops, turned back and it's been taken.

I was frantically looking for it and everyone was frustrating me with, "Are you sure it was next to you?"
"No, I thought I'd launch it to the other side of the room like it was a Discus and leave it there."

I went to the staff who also tried to imply that I'd put it somewhere strange myself. I knew I hadn't so told them to look at the CCTV and sure enough this was a precision operation: a man and woman working together. The woman swiped it and briskly made her way out of the room, once momentum had gathered she passed it back to the guy and off he went out of the venue and in to the night. It would've looked like they didn't know each other when they left if you hadn't of been privy to the goings on.

The next morning I've woken up to a text from my dad, "Were you so drunk you lost your wallet last night?"
I replied, "1.) That's bang out of order for you to assume I'd gotten pissed and lost it when there had actually been a theft.
2.) How on earth did you find that out?"

It turned out the burglars had discarded my wallet and cards in a bin a half a mile or so away outside a pub. A guy that worked at the pub had gone to put the rubbish out first thing, found them so typed 'Harriet Dyer' in to Facebook and funnily enough, the first name that came up was a Harriet Dyer that used to work with my dad in Cornwall. The guy messaged her thinking she was I, she messaged my dad to inform him of the mistaken Harriet and he messaged me. What were the chances of that?

The police were useless and nothing was done although bizarrely a few months later I got a phone call from a policeman telling me that case is closed with no resolve but then said,

"While I've got you, I don't think it's in any way related but a little bag full of tiny telephone numbers was found inside a pedophiles computer and they're all your number, can you explain that?"

"What? Absolutely not. What?"
"Hmm ok, how strange, we'll keep in touch with you about that."

They didn't and it remains probably the biggest confusion of my life.

47.) So the cycle begins again

A chap called Bovril was nice to me at the time all this was happening, he seemed like a gentleman and I appreciated that. Slight problem was he looked like my ex Gavin so it looked like I massively had a type when really it was just a coincidence.

We were at a bar ordering drinks one night and people from behind were shouting, "Gavin?" "Gavin?" trying to get Bovril's attention thinking he was Gavin.

Perhaps unknowingly I was selfish and accidentally led him on because I needed someone nice around me that looked at me like I was special; not the fucked up waste of space I felt but no matter how hard I tried to convince myself, I just didn't fancy him.

We started 'seeing' each other. He just sort of had sex with me one night, I tried to force it but there was no connection on my part but he was becoming more persistent so I sort of just let him. As he flailed on top of me like a salmon out of water I felt sad but thought,

"Well, he's still nicer than everyone else to me so I guess I'll stay with him forever."

I started getting messages from guys on Facebook about meeting up which confused me. One guy said about carrying the conversation on from Plenty of Fish. It turned out someone had made an account pretending to be me on the dating site. The profile said I only like short bald men which was a dig at Gavin and Bovril. It also said I'm incapable of really wanting a relationship because I'm only interested in my career (it was a surprise anyone got in touch with the person portrayed).

The problem I had with this Plenty of Fish page was that whoever was behind it was seeing when and where I was gigging then telling these guys to meet me at those places. I had to start opening my set by asking if anyone had come expecting a date to hopefully nip it in the bud without talking to these people. There were definitely a couple of people because they'd look shifty and then leave in the first break. I still don't know who did that, it could well come in second on the big confusion list.

48.) Then everything took a turn for the worse

I started speaking to mum less which wasn't like me. I'd put my shutters down, mentally given up.

I was gigging in London for a week so said I'd ring her loads then to catch-up but instead I ended up getting drunk then feeling too full of self pity to speak to anyone.

London was a lonely place to be feeling like that too, plus I did my trademark move where I'd arrange to stay with a friend but panic last minute about imposing on them and book a hotel with money I didn't have. Plus even at over £300 I couldn't find one anywhere near central so had to traipse near Heathrow airport every day. I'd even booked another more central place first but the confirmation email said they don't have a receptionist so I'd have to ring a number on arrival for someone to come which oddly made me panic again so I cancelled that one which lost me another £50. All in all it was quite the debacle.

Bovril turned out to be a guy "wanting nothing more than to be my friend" until it was clear that's all I wanted too and then he stopped bothering.

On the way back home from London I bought a snide Cornish pasty at the station, snide because it had peppers and sweetcorn in it and they were still trying to pass it off as Cornish! Something else wasn't right about that pasty, I felt so sick on the train back to Manchester, watery mouth and everything.

Once in Manchester I was walking the two mile journey home from the train station, was on the phone to mum and said, "Sorry mum will you excuse me for a second?" and with that I projectile vomited everywhere. Oh it was awful, like in the Rik Mayall film "Guest House Paradiso." Lots of people definitely saw me do it too, it was so loud and there was so much of it.

I was supposed to have a gig that night but couldn't do it, I needed to stay home and feel miserable. I do love to hermit which can be a vicious circle because once in that mindset it can be most difficult to vacate. One of the few things that actually helps is to vacate the premises you're hermit-ing which also feels like the worst thing to do: and that is why the circle can be vicious.

I was furious with the pasty so complained to where I bought it from, but of course it wasn't really down to that. I mentally felt I couldn't leave my flat but when there I was reminded of the horror that had happened not long previously, another relentless cycle of misery, more circles than Spirograph. I was cutting myself too then pouring bleach in the cuts so it hurt more. Of course still drinking to numb too, I couldn't see a way out.

I was very cold as my heating had stopped working because I thought it was normal to turn the boiler off every time I went to sleep like it was a lamp but this apparently caused a 'pilot light' to go out. To resolve this I got pissed, went to Poundland and bought a screwdriver kit, tinkered away with it and could safely say after that I'd done a considerable amount of further damage.

One cold morning dad rang, "Mum's not very well, if you can take some time off to come down?" I'd already taken a lot of time off and because he was being so blasé about it I didn't realise how serious it was.

"Do I need to come home?"
"Well, how many gigs have you got in?"
"Dad, how poorly is she, do I need to come home?"
"Yes, I think you should."

My friend Mick is a real character, he's always got some sort of money making scheme on the go, it's not a conversation with him if I haven't replied to what he's said with, "I'm sorry, you're importing what now?"

He was who I thought of at this time of need, which was perhaps a questionable choice as I'm sure he told me he went down a motorway the wrong way once. He does however have a heart of gold and I knew he'd drive me to Cornwall. Mick accepted the task even though he tried to get me out of the car and on to a train a few times but I wasn't having any of it, I was broken, poor and just imagining an overcrowded train was sending my anxiety through the roof.

During the journey my dad rang and he asked which train I was getting but I'd already told him twice I was getting a lift and it's not like him to not listen like that so I told him again I was getting a lift, he said everything was fine then hung up. I said to Mick, "Something's not right, my dad's being odd."

We finally got home and all that evaporated because my dad and brother were being such great company, we were all chatting and joking away with Mick when I said,

"When can I go and see mum?"
"She died"
"What?"

My legs gave way, I completely dropped to the floor, I couldn't believe it, I never got to get to her. Poor Mick was just stood there awkwardly before his mammoth trip back.

The last time I spoke to mum she said she had awful indigestion, unbeknown to everyone she'd actually had a heart attack. I told her to stop eating her dinner on the sofa!

She hadn't been eating as well as of late but she'd started to sleep in her bed (she was often in too much pain so would curl up on the sofa to sleep) and she could finally get her socks on, (rheumatism and sciatica were causing havoc with her hands and feet) we thought she was getting better but as is the way with these things sometimes it's the body's last ditch attempt at trying, a last wind if you will.

Dad thought enough was enough so called an ambulance and off they all trundled. She was going to have a full body scan so him and Joe went back home to get mum an overnight bag. Whilst they were gone the nurses decided she was too weak for the scan, her friend Theresa was with her and said she took a big breath, rolled over and then she was gone.

I wondered if during that last breath she knew it was her last? We worry so much about peoples last thoughts, who's to say it's ever reminiscent of the life they've lived / anything remotely profound? They might be more, "Gosh, I could really nibble on a block of cheese right now." Although mum wouldn't as she was lactose intolerant.

I'm so glad Theresa was there though as they were partners in crime. They once went to TK Maxx to look at handbags, left to go for a cuppa and it was then

Theresa realised she had a left arm full of handbags she'd been draping on herself whilst looking.

Dad said when they got back it was so quiet and still with mum lying there lifeless. It seemed everything had stopped where they were but beyond the curtain they were sectioned off by was the hustle and bustle of everything else; it almost seemed unjust that everything was even allowed to carry on.

I went to see her the next morning and of course it's something I'll never forget, her just there, not alive anymore. I kissed her, she was so cold, it was all so very sad.

When you lose someone suddenly, well whenever really we naturally focus on our last interaction with them and whether we got to say goodbye which is often actually for our own peace of mind rather than theirs. Really you need to ask, "Were you a massive dick to them whilst they were alive?" If yes, well they probably saw you for what you were then so please work on being a nicer person moving forward, and if no, please don't beat yourself up about it, they would've known you were a good egg.

Mum was a very proud Yorkshire woman, she stopped being able to breath properly but wouldn't do anything about it. Her head could've dropped off and instead of calling an ambulance (which someone else would've had to do actually due to the lack of head being problematic) she'd order someone to go to

Holland and Barratt to get her some cod liver oil tablets. She wouldn't be told and hated prescription drugs because of the side affects and not knowing what was in them so preferred to refer to the book, "Foods That Harm, Foods That Heal."

She opted for calcium tablets and I will say this, just because something is natural please do still do your research because the paramedics that came round said that even though natural they can still cause a build up of calcium on your heart which could've played a part in it all.

Joe came home to get changed to then go back out with his girlfriend to the cinema so he carried guilt that he should've realised something was wrong instead of going back out but again, she was a proud old goose that wouldn't let anyone help her.

If you're reading this and you fall in the category of "proud goose" (whether old or otherwise) we get it - You don't like a fuss but can you please see it another way for a second: if there truly is something wrong and heaven forbid something happens but you were resilient in anyone helping you

1.) Needing a little bit of help is most certainly not causing a fuss
2.) Surely "causing a fuss" is better than dying?
3.) Imagine how shit it is for the people that thought you had indigestion when it was a heart attack. Although not doctors it is mortifying because

one would think it'd be easy enough to differentiate between the two.

"Doctor, doctor I think I'm having a heart attack"
"Not a problem at all - Here, have a Rennie."

49.) Come together right now, over she

My dad is unsympathetic when it comes to anyone taking any days off work so encouraged Joe to go to work the next day. Of course he turned up broken, was asked what was wrong and the moment he said why they said, "Why on earth are you here?" and sent him home.

The funeral was going to be a couple of weeks: because she died so suddenly there had to be an inquest so dad encouraged me to honour the gigs I had in, the first being on halloween weekend. I spoke to Joe about it, "Forget what he says, you know if you're up to it or not and it's totally understandable if you're not." I said I didn't want to be around drunk people dressed up as dead people and we decided that was fair enough.

Dad, Joe and I became an inseparable little team. Joe and I had spells of getting along although overall we'd bicker and argue but the moment mum died that evaporated, ever since we've gotten on ever so well.

After the inquest we thought we'd finally be able to get the funeral sorted but alas that was still not to be because every person that worked at the funeral directors decided to go to Budapest to see Michael

Bublé in concert. One would think at a place there's always going to be custom no matter what, there'd at least be one person left to hold fort. Also on the tour there was a fucking Plymouth date.

In true Cornwall style of course we knew the funeral directors, my brother went to school with the grandsons of the people who owned it which was nice actually as I think they were extra sympathetic which was what we needed. Well, once back from rocking out to Bublé they were.

At one point the funeral director was taking notes about what we wanted when she herself started crying which I thought was a bit much especially as she took the tissues from me. She said it was nice we all agreed on everything as apparently that's not very common. Think how many funerals she does, I bet that's the worst bit; families bickering about what they get and how the funeral is supposed to be. I'd rather dead bodies any day of the week than having to deal with the alive ones.

She asked if we wanted a ring that was on mums finger to which dad replied, "No it's ok" before I could say anything. After about ten minutes I plucked up the courage to say, "Sorry, I really would like her ring actually, if that would be ok?" She said, "Of course" and started crying again, using up all the remaining tissues.

I'm so glad I spoke up, I know I would've regretted it for ever if I didn't. It's such a delicate little ring that she never took off so I feel closer to her just having it.

Mum wasn't religious so we compiled the perfect bespoke for her funeral, it really was exactly how she would've wanted and that's exactly how it should be. So many people have funerals that are no reflection on the person that's departed, it becomes less a celebration of them and more a celebration of whatever religion it is the people still alive have chosen for them.

Ours was simple, Joe picked a song then said a few words, I picked a song and said a few words then Dad picked a song and said a few words. When I say, "A few words" anyone that knows us knows a few words is more likely a few thousand.

We sorted out our songs then dad said I should go to Scotland to do a gig that was deemed quite important as it was even now was still a few weeks until the funeral. I was so empty. Mum died on the 26th October 2014 which was the day the clocks went back so the worst day in my whole life had an extra fucking hour to it.

I never adjusted my watch again, figured it'll always eventually sort itself out which was all very well and good but didn't help with gigging. This first gig back I turned up over an hour early and couldn't understand why no-one was letting me in so was knocking on the office door; eventually a lady appeared and snapped at me that it wasn't time yet so I sort of bewilderedly floated away like the hollow carcass of a lady I was.

When it was actual time for the gig the tech for the venue was outside writing on a sandwich board for the show, he asked if I was ok and I replied by hysterically crying in the street.

The show actually went amazing which was great as it was being recorded for radio. I told all the acts from the off what had happened (because I'd been scooped in from the street sobbing by the bewildered technician) and everyone was lovely, I actually had such a laugh which I wasn't expecting. I did feel like I was having an outer body experience whilst onstage though and was above looking down on myself (from a great height, not as in a negative fashion, like usual) if that makes sense?

Time to head back to Cornwall for the funeral.

The people mum worked with weren't on the same page as her. Her cleaning job at the cinema was supposed to start at 8:00am, those were the hours the job description stated. That didn't suit a lady she worked with (remember the lady on the bus that used to get people to shout, "Skinny bitch" at my mum whilst she did the school run? Well, it was her my mum was now working with) so she made a fuss and got everyone to start at 6:00am instead.

It ground mum down because she wasn't sleeping well anyway so just as she was drifting off to sleep, she was having to get up again as it was up at 5:00am to get to work for 6:00am.

After she had the stroke she felt pressured to go back probably before she was ready because the general consensus by her colleagues was that she'd already had more than enough time off.

She was unable to put up with it any longer and had actually retired for a year before she passed away. I couldn't wait for her to get her quality of life back but bizarrely her body must've been confused by the sudden rest and started to develop these ailments that we've since been told were probably a delayed result of the stroke she had all those years previous.

When she died the 'Skinny bitch shouter' rang up asking about the funeral to which I said, "Now do you believe she was ill?" She laughed. Just laughed. I didn't tell her about the funeral as mum wouldn't have wanted her there as the sort of person she was she wouldn't have been there because she cared but because she'd want to gossip to people about what it was like.

The only dick that slipped through the net at the funeral was the manager of the cinema that she didn't particularly like, it seemed for him it was a case of him "Being seen to be there" which is for the company, not my lovely mother, I should've frog marched him out. She genuinely got on well with the actual owner too so he would have been more than welcome to come instead - Send the organ grinder, not the creepy little monkey.

As everyone was entering we played Cold Plays' Fix You (she was a big fan of Coldplay which I guess was her only flaw. Also now I'm typing this, how bleak is it to play "Fix You" at a funeral when there's literally no fixing them).

Joe picked Cat Stevens - Morning has Broken
I picked Neil Young - Heart of Gold
Dad picked Leonard Cohen - That's no way to say goodbye.

As everyone was leaving we played OMD - Electricity. It was perfect.

My exact words…

It's easy to just assume that everything will always be how it always has been. I never envisaged the last few weeks. Prior to this I think I took for granted that mum would always be there.

I feel lost without her and hope she knew that even though I didn't live by her side in Cornwall I've never loved anyone more.

I hate the phrase "One in a million" because I think people use it far too freely and the "One in a million" is usually a dunderhead called Dave that can drink his own bodyweight in Jagerbombs on a Saturday night along with all the other "One in a million's." My mum was definitely one in a million.

I've never met someone so selfless, kind and honest. She'd do anything she could for the people she loved (well even the people she didn't love) and never put herself first. I wish she would have a bit more often, but that made her who she was — With her heart of gold.

Mum was also the funniest person I've ever met. Her sense of humour was dry, quick and often unexpected. I'd always describe her as a 'slow burner' because she'd initially seem a bit shy if she didn't know you but once comfortable, being around her and the things she came out with was priceless.

I remember coming home from work at TK Maxx one day and mum's standing in the front room with a massive stick and I was like, "What you doing with that?" She goes, "I thought we could play limbo tonight!"

She had her trademark dressing gown that became her favourite attire, although quite frankly illogical because she wore it because she got the sweats.

I'd love it when the pair of us would sit on a sofa each with our matching dressing gowns on and natter about all the latest gossip, then she'd hint that she wanted a cuppa and then I'd say, "Ok, I'll make you a flipping cuppa!" And she'd go, "Only if you're making one."

She loved a cup of tea. I don't think I've ever met anyone that drank as much tea in all my life. Herbal tea is trendy now but Mrs Dyer was drinking it from way back when. She epitomised the English tradition of any problem will be solved with a cup of tea. "Help, my leg needs to be amputated!" "Not a problem, I'll put the kettle on."

Our Christmas's together were my favourite times, I'm sad that we won't have another but happy that all four of us were together for the last. We'd always underestimate her when it came to board games etc but she always surprised us. My mother was ever so wise.

I was 30 last year but mum would still creep into my room with a sack in the middle of the night whilst I was sleeping and we'd all pretend Santa had been. Mum found such fun in the most innocent of things. She was also a joy to buy presents for as she was always so grateful.

I'll miss mine and Joe's tradition of getting together with our ideas and going shopping for her. She was also so quirky and her favourite present one year was a vintage jammy dodger biscuit badge that we got for her. She wore it with such pride. Most people would've found it ridiculous.

One year we got her a foot spa and we saved it for a New Year's Eve to stay in and have a girly night. We turned it on and then pottered upstairs to get our dressing gowns. We came back down and the whole room was filled with suds. I was an idiot and had put soapy liquid in instead of oils, then whacked it on full blast. We giggled away.

Mum hadn't had it easy. There was always some obstacle or another in her way and she was so unlucky. I'd say to her that because she was a genuinely lovely person something wonderful would one day happen for her and I was sure of that.

This didn't quite happen but I'm so glad she's not in any pain anymore because she'd been in pain for quite a long time now. It's heartbreaking that she worked for so long and then wasn't allowed to enjoy her retirement after she'd been anticipating it for so long.

She was such a support to everyone that knew her. I felt that she was always with me on my travels as I'd ring her from all over the country for a little natter. She always knew what to say. Even though I live by myself, I felt like I had a housemate because she was always just the other end of the phone if need be. Sometimes I'd lie on my bed and put the phone on the pillow next to mine whilst chatting so it felt like she was actually there with me chatting.

My mum also had the patience of a saint (she'd have to being married to dad) I'd like to finish my reading by reading a poem that she helped me learn for an assembly when I was at primary school. Whatever play or show I was in she'd always help me learn my lines and de-stress me from insisting that I couldn't do it.

Poem — Good Company, Leonard Clark

I'm so glad she was my mum and I got to have with her the time I did, for that I am grateful. Thank you.

It's heartbreaking that towards the end of her life I didn't speak to her as much as I usually would have as "I had my own shit going on." I didn't want to bother her and no doubt she didn't want to bother me and as a result we were both most probably very bothered.

I could be difficult, so up and down and when I did see her I was guilty of sometimes paying more attention to my stupid phone than her. We as a society are great at having not seen the people we are with in an age then spending that time with them trying to communicate with people we aren't with and actually hold in far less regard.

To those still lucky enough to have both / a parent /
relative / carer - SEE THEM MORE and when you arrive
turn your phone off, leave it in an other room and go
and be present with people that matter the most.
Nothing else is more important.

Part of me definitely departed the day mum did. One
gets on because quite possibly the alternative is
worse but a void's been flapping wide open ever
since.

50.) When life gives you lemons - Get your brain checked once and for all

I'm not sure I ever would've got help for my mental illness whilst my mum was alive and that's nothing against her, in fact it's another thing that was lovely about her, she'd never think there was anything wrong with my brain because she thought I was great just the way I am. Lovely, but doing nothing to distinguish inner trauma.

Now she wasn't around the obvious thing for me to do was kill myself but the problem with that was I'd only just seen first hand how heartbreaking sorting out a funeral was and couldn't do that to dad and Joe so soon. The financial side of it too, no-one had the money for two funerals on the trot.

My pal Sheila felt this could well be the thing to teeter me over the edge and was close to a company of counsellors so hooked me up which was good of her, of course the noise in my mind was still there in Dolby surround sound though so off I went to see a doctor once again but this time intent on following instruction. The doctor reiterated a bipolar based spiel which when listening about it all properly did actually make sense and If there was any way to make the lodger between my ears an easier house guest I was all in, in fact this time I was so in that it felt liberating to accept it all. I finally took the prescribed medication which made me feel stoned at first but I welcomed it; everything quietened, the stormy seas that had been raging slowly started to calm.

Doing things my way if it could be called a way hadn't worked so it was time for change. I'm not going to lie and say it was 100% better straight away, there were definitely some negatives to the medication I was put on…

1.) I could shit myself at any moment
2.) I kept seeing imaginary mice scuttle on past.
3.) Even though I welcomed most numbness I found myself to be numb sexually too so couldn't climax

It was still a battle but now there was a new feeling bubbling within, to do mum proud.

51.) Friends

Clive and Gemma were a couple (neither were football hooligans which was nice) that thought it best I move in with them as they didn't think I should be by myself, we got on well and they seemed concerned so I didn't see why not.

I had to cancel a lot of work due to being in a state, helping sort funeral etc, was in Cornwall a lot so funds were haemorrhaging. I moved out of my flat only to be charged with a load of damages that of course were nothing to do with me but entirely to do with MC, a parting gift.

I'll always be grateful for them putting me up and when I came back up from the funeral, Clive drove all the way to Birmingham train station from Manchester (as it was much cheaper for me to get a train to there from Cornwall) to pick me up to take back to theirs. Once there they put on a little birthday party as my birthday had been and gone since I was away which was so kind.

It was Clive's birthday a few weeks after so we had another party at the house, quite a few comedy friends came but Gemma was only there for a couple of hours as she had to head to Cumbria for something the following day. The later it got the more of a mess

Clive became and he lifted me up on top of his lap which was strange and too familiar but we didn't speak of it again, after all we were all getting along so well. By the end of the night I was so drunk too and ended up snogging one of our mutual comedy friends.

I came to realise that after a few weeks Clive and Gemma expected me to be over my mum dying.

I'd always liked a drink, they knew that, we'd all been out drinking lots together. Admittedly I've had a tempestuous relationship with it but I've had more of one with people, so many have been and gone: alcohol has been the constant that hasn't, has stuck around without the judgment… was how I saw it at the time. Also since probably around 2010 it's never been spirits, just a few beers or red wine.

First came their judgement, "But you don't have any money" A tenner here and there for beers is making no difference, I'm an adult, whichever way I want to grieve I'm going to do it, I didn't ask for you to take me in, you did.

Their relationship was also hard to be around so I wanted to either go out and it was winter so nice to be in a pub or stay in and be numb when I was in their company.

There was no trust because they went out with each other when they were younger and he'd cheated on her with her best friend. They got back together years later but the trust never fully restored.

The room I was staying in was next to the bathroom, Gemma wouldn't let him have a bath in peace. I'd hear her scratching at the door then squawking, "Baaaaaaaaby." She'd go in and I'd hear whinging, whining then them doing baby voices at each other. I think if anyone that isn't a baby does a baby voice they should have to give birth through their nostrils.

There started to be an atmosphere between us which turned out to be that even though they said I could stay as long as I wanted and didn't have to worry about money they decided without letting me know that this wasn't enough as their heating bill had gone up. I was getting food for the flat daily and the bill had gone up because it was their first winter there, nothing to do with me because I was sitting in the freezing cold when they weren't in for that exact reason, and because I couldn't figure out how to turn the blasted thing on!

The bill I understood when was a bit higher was the water bill because I often did the dishes else they wouldn't be done. The moment I was told about this of course I gave them money, all the situation needed was communication but instead they told our mutual friends I was causing problems which wasn't helpful.

A month or so after mums death Bovril tried to make an effort and asked if he could take me out for a catchup which I thought was nice of him. We both got so drunk though, I ended up confessing all my childhood shite, topped that off with a hysterical cry about mum and he reacted by snogging me then pulling away to tell me it was wrong again and again. It was a mess, then in my drunken state I thought I'd make it all better by sucking his dick.

Gemma was holier than thou about that too - In fact that one was fair enough, I was bang out of order for doing that in her living room.

The biggest love in my world wasn't there any more so off I was looking for something, anything as some sort of substitution but as per usual was looking was in all the wrong places.

There was a guy on Tinder I was chatting to before mum passed so obviously I went quiet when that happened but eventually came back, was really honest with what had happened and gave him a get out of jail card by saying, "I totally understand if that's too much to deal with for you" but he stuck with me, seemed really nice actually. We arranged to meet but on the day he asked if we could rearrange because he'd been called into work which seemed totally believable, "Of course, no worries, let me know when you want to re-schedule." I heard nothing from him ever again, well and truly ghosted. No-one's cares if you're not that into us, these things happen, just be honest, let us know where we stand. He knew what I was going through, was given a chance to "get out" but instead behaved like an absolute stink-fish.

I needed to vacate this other toxic relationship I'd managed to set up residence in.

Gemma said my presence was making her anxious but again didn't think to talk about it at the time with me and when she finally did she opened with, "Here's the problem we have with you…" and said what I've already mentioned like the drinking. She also kept saying, "We only put you up because we knew that's what you'd do for us,"

"Let me tell you this, I fucking wouldn't!"

52.) Lady pad

I was desperate to leave. One day I was talking to another comedian (Rusty) about my living situation and he suggested perhaps flat sharing with a lovely girl Lizzy that lived with him and his girlfriend (he was with Beatrice). Sorry if all the names are confusing, I'm aware there's so many to try and keep track of, I've even tried to narrow them down as much as possible.

I really got on with Lizzy, thought it was a great idea so asked her about it. To my surprise this caused an issue as telling her that Rusty suggested us living together made her feel like he didn't want her where she was anymore.

Eventually Lizzy said she wanted to move in with me but would find it difficult to view places as she didn't have any time at present. I asked if she was sure she was up for it and then as I was desperate asked if she minded if I found somewhere really nice could we just move in? She agreed, she honestly could've said no as that would have been perfectly understandable.

It's worth mentioning too that finding a place to rent when you're self-employed is an absolute ball-ache because landlords obviously want an easy life so a tenant with the same income each month, not the unpredictable funds of a travelling clown. I showed Lizzy the details of one place, she said it was really nice. It was a private landlord who was a writer that understood self-employed woes, the flat was modern and walking distance to the city centre, perfect. As I'd already asked about moving straight in if I found somewhere good and she'd agreed - Upon viewing it I, perhaps a little impulsively said, "Where do I sign?"

This did not go down well. I think Lizzy was airing concerns to Beatrice but not to me, not to be a dick though, because she didn't want to upset anyone. So then to Beatrice it looked like I was perhaps taking advantage.

As I was leaving the couples retreat Gemma asked if we could meet up soon, I looked at her in disbelief, "I think it's best if we have a bit of space?" She went on about how she hoped I wouldn't let them become distant when they were the only ones that took me in. Do you hear that? Carol Vorderman's on the phone wanting to give you a Pride Of Britain Award.

It was great to be in a new place, soon after I moved in Lizzy did, well I say she did but it was her parents that moved her in. They were now in the flat often which was a surprise, especially because some times she wasn't, it was just me and them. I felt like I'd moved out for freedom but had now managed to super impose myself into a family that wasn't even mine.

They were there hanging up pictures, repeatedly washing curtains etc, the amount of bleach they got through was unbelievable; they were carrying on like the flat was absolute filth when there was nothing wrong with it, I half expected them to rock up in full hazmat suits, looking for E.T.

Lizzy's mum even looked like 'Aggie' from Kim and Aggie's 'How Clean Is Your House,' although she wasn't best pleased I told her that. She started to interrogate me on how I was going to behave around her daughter which I found confusing and started to retrace my steps to establish when exactly it was that I'd asked for her daughters hand in marriage.

Another time she asked me so many questions about my mum that I started to cry to which she said, "I never bothered crying over my mum."

When it was Lizzy and I we had such a laugh. Lizzy definitely had mental health issues but felt unjust in having them, which of course leads to more. We definitely bonded in both struggling with that side of things.

Beatrice and Rusty's relationship was not in a good place, now I think about it I think perhaps Beatrice seemingly not best pleased with Lizzy moving out was partly down to that too.

Beatrice would often shout at Rusty in public whilst he stood there gormless not saying anything which led me to not think to question his behaviour.

I genuinely don't think Beatrice even realised at the time, I only see it now looking back but there were big feelings for another guy in their friendship group (Mo.) The way she looked at him was how one could only hope to be looked at one day: she found everything he said and did hilarious but her boyfriend an irritant. It was Mo I'd drunkenly snogged at Clive's birthday soiree, things were already not great between Beatrice and I but after that they really suffered.

Beatrice and I would always travel to gigs together because we were good friends, she drove, I didn't and I only lived about a ten minute drive from her. We were both doing a gig together but this time she said if I wanted a lift I was to meet her at her house which even though only a ten minute drive way is roughly an hour walk and nightmare via public transport as you've got to go into the city centre to come back out again plus there's now an atmosphere between us, another comic was coming, I felt down and vulnerable so I decided to make my own way there.

At the gig once they arrived I felt there was now an atmosphere with the other act too. I'm a naturally paranoid person so even as I'm writing this I'm like,

"Was I just being paranoid?" but there was no denying this atmosphere, it was awful.

I felt once again alcohol was the only thing there for me. There were free drinks at the gig so I was drinking can after can after can. "Bloody hell Harriet, how many of those have you put away?" exclaimed one of the other acts. "As many as I fucking well want to."

Lizzy and I had been minding Beatrice and Rusty's cat: it sat on my lasagne and was a massive diva. I told my brother and he joked that I should write a suicide note pretending to be from it, I foolishly told Beatrice this at the gig panicking because of the atmosphere, was drunk and thought it could be some sort of ice breaker between us but couldn't have been more wrong, she was disgusted and looked at me like I was threatening to kill her cat. I'm not sure what I was thinking to be honest.

The gig was in the middle of nowhere and by the time it had finished it was so late; Beatrice didn't offer a lift back but that was fine because I was done. I waited at a train station that was practically a field for over an hour, I ran out of tobacco too (but that wasn't anyone else's fault but my own) and as I sat there crying into my filter tips it started to rain, "Why the fuck would I want to be alive? Why didn't I buy tobacco earlier?"

I eventually got home, told Lizzy what had happened who said I must have confused the issues with Beatrice which at the time made me want to shake her.

Friendships shouldn't be so difficult. As I worked with these people it started to feel like even comedy, the hopeful thing in my life was again beginning to lose its shine again.

I needed to meet up with Beatrice as I didn't feel there was reason for any beef. "I've got no time to meet until April" was her response, we were in January, I had to bother her to meet me earlier. We finally got a date in, I turn up, she arrives and starts with small talk, "No, we've come here to talk about something in particular, let's get this squashed." This whatever it was had gone on for far too long, it couldn't be in my headspace any longer.

She said, "The way I see it is a lot of my friends are upset and the common denominator in that is you" which said all I needed to know.

I will say here that sometimes when people are big into feminism they need to reassess their responses to things because Bovril and Mo were her dearest friends and none of their behaviour was ever questioned when Beatrice knew all I'd been through.

Things were squashed after that - I didn't have the mental capacity for any more, but I had to emotionally check out to a certain degree with everyone, done were the days of me socialising, I only really spoke with Lizzy because we lived together, too many people had disappointed me since mums death.

I'd been going to the counselling sessions Sheila had sorted out for me, I'd also done a gig for them to raise money for their services so became to know them a bit personally too which in hindsight perhaps marred the waters. One counsellor definitely had a drink problem and another was in her 30s but had married a 65 year old so judgementally on my part I felt a bit like, "Who were they to help get my shit together when theirs doesn't seem to be?" Perhaps I was just making excuses, although when I finally used up all my pre-ambling and opened up properly in sessions I was told, "It's all very dramatic" which I'm not sure was helpful.

53.) New man on the block

A guy I used to chat to years previously messaged me out of the blue on Facebook. We first came in to contact on a dating site but never met because things had started with Gavin so as a result I stopped all correspondence with him.

I really felt things could be on the up with him getting back in touch, perhaps he was, "The one that got away" if there was such a thing.

We met up, went bowling, had a great time then he kept mentioning coming to mine after. Why would he if he didn't want *that*? Perhaps because of my past I've slept with people because I've felt it's what's been expected but on this occasion I hadn't had sex in a couple of years (I know it probably doesn't seem like that the way I'm writing all this - It's a tricky endeavour trying to fit ones whole life into a certain amount of words so I'm condensing more than it probably seems) so we slept together but afterwards he sort of made out that I'd hoodwinked him in to it although there were no signs of him feeling like that as it was happening.

He asked about my mum and I started to sob which was just what the situation was missing, by now it had still only been six months. He said that's the side of me he liked and wanted to see more of but then when I opened up about other stuff it'd scare him off. That day he saw my bipolar medication by my bed and asked what it was for, I'm open enough so told him to which he replied,

"Does that mean if I stayed over you'd murder me in the night?"
"It didn't…."

He was another head-fuck. He had all these rules and preconceptions of what he should want but what he did was contradictory. He liked the idea of being with someone but didn't have the emotional capacity to think of anyone other than himself. His mind games were so subtle that I never knew where I stood but was alway led to believe anything negative I felt was a result of my own manifestation.

At first we messaged all day every day, we got on so well, had a laugh, he was so complimentary too. After weeks he told me that he couldn't imagine his life without me now. I of course believed this because, well what do people gain from lying about such?

He told me I should get some nice underwear for when we next meet, I was gigging where he lived for a few days so was staying at a hotel there. I'm sure we arranged to meet early afternoon but when I got there and messaged him he told me that was never the plan, that I'd gotten muddled. He made an appearance that evening and was on about it being a test to see if we could talk to each other without having to sleep together. We ended up sleeping together, if I'm sporting underwear that he's suggested is that not pretty inevitable? He was supposed to be staying over but left which made me feel worthless. I refused to partake in another merry dance of mind-games and tests so said, "Let's just cool whatever this is and keep it just as friends."

Once again I was gigging not too far from where he lived so arranged to meet at the gig as friends.
He turned up late, was really rude about the comedy on because it wasn't mainstream then told me he wanted to take me in to the bathroom near where we were chatting and bend me over the sink which I found to be very mixed signals. After the gig I travelled back with some of the other acts and the next morning I woke up to a load of pictures he'd texted me of my own zoomed in face that he'd got from scrolling through hundreds of pictures on my Facebook profile with comments saying I used to look like Paris Hilton! He was very shallow so I think he was perhaps trying to justify to himself fancying me by comparing me to someone famous?

He kept saying we weren't in a relationship but then was trying to meet, then not trying to meet. Talking to my counsellor about it made me realise whether he wanted to accept it or not we were in a relationship of sorts - Albeit a chaotic one.

I was gigging in Wales for a couple of days, he was going to come on the last day to a show, then we were going to spend the last night in a luxury hotel that I'd sorted out (Jesus Harriet, take a hint) but on the day he was supposed to be coming all communication ceased, then an hour or so before he was supposed to arrive he said he wasn't coming then radio silence, not a sorry about how I'd lose the money on the hotel or anything. A day or so later he messaged saying he'd had some awful news to do with his health and because of how he'd been carrying on my first thought was, "Oh gosh he's got aids" but after hours of trying to weasel it out of him he told me tests have shown there *could* be a chance he *could* develop diabetes. I'm not downplaying or disrespecting anyone that's diabetic but it's very manageable these days, really not the end of the world and he'd been told there was a small chance he COULD get it.

It's guys like him that regularly throw about such gems as, "Women are all the same" and "They're all mental" but it's their confusing behaviour that causes us to question and perhaps not trust which is actually the fitting way to respond to the actions they've provided. Treat people how you'd want to be treated, end of. The man ban had resumed.

54.) Business

There's so much more to comedy than, "Just being funny" there's loads of admin and a lot of 'business' that isn't show.

I did my Edinburgh Fringe debut hour too soon, colleagues spent years previewing their debut shows because they had their eye on the prize and they're lying if they say they didn't.

The prize being a nomination for what used to be the Perrier awards which is basically an acknowledgement from a group of people that matter in the industry that you're doing something right, definitely flavour of the month and if you don't have an agent or are a shoo-in for TV work that's likely to be about to change, the door is now ajar.

My thoughts are always jumping from one thing to the next and with my debut hour I had a lifetime of mental illness I was trying to deal with whilst also trying to process latest MC dealings. By the end of it my brain had already started to map out another show, something far removed from all the above.

I've never been tested for ADHD but anyone that knows me seems to think I have it. Just last week two people that work with adults with ADHD for the NHS messaged me after seeing me do Facebook live streams telling me they think I've clearly got it.

The agent I had at the time of my debut hour produced shows so it was assumed they'd produce mine. I might as well of set fire to over 5K. A new girl started working for them, I'd never met anyone so posh but shouldn't judge and was told to give her a chance as she'd moved up from London and didn't know anyone but no matter how hard I tried I just couldn't warm to her and she never gave Manchester a chance, all she did was slag it off. If I did meet up with her she'd monologue about herself until it was time to depart, never ask how anyone else was and when I set up a WhatsApp group with her and a few others to do stuff because she was lonely she got agitated because it was tricky for some of us to make plans because she had a day job but everyone else were comedians so worked evenings.

As it was my first solo show I wanted to do it properly but didn't have a clue about the 'business side' of comedy so felt a fish out of water. One thing I did know was everyone that does well at the festival seems to have PR. I asked El' Posho who I needed to get in touch with about getting PR and she said,

"Don't you worry about that, that's what I used to do with my old job, I'll do it."
"Oh wow really? Are you sure?"
"Absolutely."

As Edinburgh became nearer nothing was mentioned but like I said, I didn't really know how it all worked so naively assumed it was getting sorted. As my dad says, "Never assume."

Since 2014 so many shows have touched on mental health as a subject but this was one of the first so there was a lot to push but nothing other than what I'd sorted myself seemed to be happening so I popped in to see them (probably later than I should have because I didn't want to bother anyone) to see what they were doing and what they needed to be doing, they told me they were busy. Then I was told, "El Posho nearly got a broadsheet into your show the other day" like I should be grateful, "Congratulations on nearly doing your job."

Embarrassingly I then waited until after the fringe to show them the email exchange in which I was told my PR would be sorted and they said, "Thanks for not bringing it up in Edinburgh as it was such a stressful time." Yes, but you were being paid to have a stressful time whereas I was paying to have a stressful time of which if you'd have just done what you said you would or told me from the off that you couldn't none of this would be an issue.

I resented them for not reducing how much they were charging me after mistakes were made. After the festival we had meetings and that but the way I saw them had changed because of seeing how they do

business and what they were charging against the work
they were doing.

55.) Turning a negative into a positive

In the end that's what the show ended up being, talking through the process of where I was at with my mental illness and that's one positive I did actually get from it all - How other people responded to talking about mental health so openly via comedy. People would come up to me after they'd watched the show wanting to talk about their own mental health issues and would say hearing me talking about it so openly made them feel they could now carry that on with others. One girl came with her sister and told me they'd had quite a complex relationship where she felt she couldn't talk openly about her mental health issues but watching my show together had opened up a long overdue conversation.

Obviously it wasn't for everyone, some people believe depression etc is a choice so I got some telling me that and some even trying to recruit me in to a religious cult. One chap I thought was a super fan as he came to watch the show every day but it turned out he was homeless and I was the only person that wouldn't kick him out.

I decided when the festival was over I didn't want the conversation and openness to end and at the exact time to me feeling this it was reported in the media how comedians tend to be the most prone performers to mental illness (Tears of a Clown and all that) so I came up with the idea to start a monthly comedy night in Manchester where comedians do material / tell stories about their mental illness in a bid to raise awareness but in a different way, a fun way. It seemed to appeal to people that suffer / have suffered with mental illness and quickly the night seemed to muster quite the collection of lovely supporters. As it stemmed from doing my show, 'Barking at Aeroplanes' I called it, 'Barking Tales.'

It was a safe space for people where the usual comedy night set-up might not be appealing due to the potential of being spoken to which can be anxiety inducing especially if spoke to in an aggressive manner as is unfortunately sometimes the way. I did a weekend gig before lockdown and the compere called a load of women in the audience "Slags" and then brought me on. Perfect.

I'm the compere of mine and will tend to only speak to people if they've spoken to me first or if they've been coming for years and we've built that rapport, I can categorically say no-one's ever been called a slag on my watch.

There's a Meetup Group (Meetup is an online site for people looking to meet new people, get out etc) in Manchester called 'Socially Awkward Meetup group' and a lot of people that come to the night are from there.

The regulars have a special place in my heart now, I consider a lot of them dear friends, it's something I look forward to and where I can totally be myself, it really is a safe space. When people come, like it and come back again, there's no better feeling. I guess because it's such a niche quiche if you do like it chances are you'll be cavorting through our door on the regular, but if not oh sweet Jesus, what a shambolic mess where a woman has a rambling breakdown onstage for far too long every month. Of course the shambolic mess is I.

I had a meeting with a guy from the BBC about turning the night into a radio special. A lot of the regulars would be included as so many of them have such interesting tales to tell, more so than a lot of the comedians to be honest. A lot of them have been let down by the system, what some of them have been through really makes you stop and assess why you're such a whiny bastard.

One guy was agoraphobic, would drive to the gig but would never make it out of his car, one day he did and became a regular. Once a wonderful act, Harriet (Kemsley) just in case you think I'm talking about myself in third person which the audience did when she first did the night and these are people that know me well. Anyway Harriet was onstage, talking about her dyspraxia saying she read a book on it whilst she was on holiday and it turned out the professor that wrote the book she read was in the audience. How great is that?

One thing that wasn't quite so good was Harriet asked if anyone had ever had chlamydia, one girl said she had so Harriet assumed like anyone would that she would've got it the same way as most people would; being a bit more sexually promiscuous when younger but this was a girl that had been trafficked and was very open about it so everyone in the room knew that it would've been due to that so made for brief uncomfortableness from everyone apart from Harriet as she was oblivious, and the girl it happened to as she like I said is open about it, and autistic which makes it near impossible to ignore a question especially if it applies. But that's the beauty of the night, everyone can be exactly how they are.

I was sick of hearing month in, month out about how government cuts affect the regulars and the benefits they need. So many of them aren't up to working but of course are told they are and these companies in which they work for have no empathy or lenience in their rules for people with mental illness. Dmitry became a regular, he was cantankerous but charming in his own way, he was definitely victim to that and hanged himself.

Such a small gesture but I felt this BBC show could give people like Dmitry a voice, show how mental illness really is, something raw, real and beyond middle class people adopting an edge for a profitable selling point.

I get that the BBC have to be cautious about a lot of things especially since they housed the career of a prolific pedophile for so long but this guys comments were, "Umm, how do we know that these people would be of sound mind when agreeing to something like this?" and, "The best thing to do would be to probably make them all sit at the back" so their night wouldn't be theirs any more, great.

That agent I had involved himself in to the correspondence the more interest increased which I assumed was a good thing until he in correspondence with the guy from BBC started asking really basic questions about the night that someone representing me should definitely already know. I emailed him privately saying,

"You really should have come to this night by now so you'd know what you're helping to pitch? It's been going for well over a year now and you haven't been once."

"But I've just had baby."
"But I didn't have your baby."
"Sorry if you're in a mood with me"

"In a mood with you?" This is business, of which you're usually the first to point out to me. I'm supposed to go easy on you because "you've" just had a kid but you're still charging me a ridiculous amount of money for half arsed jobs? Do kindly fuck off.

Also I remember him saying, "You need to find us stuff too" That's your job! Off I departed with the want to do it all myself, I'd done everything myself up until then and often felt redundant leaving them to do things anyway. It was infuriating when mistakes were then made with things that I was more than capable doing myself, was happy to do myself but was paying them to do. One girl had left over a year previously and her mistakes were still making themselves known.

The agent hugged me as I arrived to tell him things weren't working, I informed him of my plan to depart and when I left he didn't hug me goodbye, in fact he was quite sulky which confirmed I'd made the right decision.

56.) New member of the lady pad

Lizzy's parent's bought her a house so she was moving out to live in that. She was sad to be leaving and I was sad to see her go, we got on well and understood each other. The only thing I struggled with sometimes was I'd always try to make her feel better but her only setting was to think she was capable of nothing so would be on autopilot in just dismissing anything nice that was said, "That's very kind of you, thank you" was always her go to reply which was said in such a hollow way that I knew she wasn't entertaining it for a second. She had such little confidence in herself which I totally understand but you have to keep hold of a little pipette of hope, if there's no hope there's nothing.

I put an ad on Spareroom to find someone for her room. A girl asked to look around, it started out very hopeful because she knew a comedian I knew and she greeted me with a Terry's Chocolate Orange but it got bizarre quick - She started by telling me how she kept hooking up with guys on Tinder which raised alarm bells. Are you going to bring men that you don't know into my home willy nillily? That's dangerous, careless and selfish as it holds no regard to who you're living with, come on now, we're not at university any more.

She was so materialistic too, driven by money.

"I'm a nurse."
"Fantastic, that's what I'd want to be if I didn't do comedy, it must be so tough but so rewarding?"
"I hate it, I'm only doing it until I find someone wealthy so I don't have to work any more."

I laughed thinking she was joking but she was serious.

I have no patience with shit like that, it's fucking depressing, no mention of love or any qualities she'd be looking for other than money. Being paid to be with someone is nothing short of an in-house escort.

She was on domination / bondage sites which I naively didn't even know existed until meeting her - Although that's a naivety I can get onboard with. She said how she answered an advert from a guy with a lot of money that wanted to take her to dinner and she was to be entirely submissive.

He chose her entire outfit for her from lingerie to shoes to dress, she put it all on and waited for the car he was sending. The car took her to some very expensive restaurant. He spoke of a girl that had "ruined his life," they lost their virginity to each other but she'd apparently used him then said they couldn't be together anymore.

She wasn't sure about him but then he started ordering the priciest items on the menu which piqued her interest. At one point as a waiter went past she asked him for a glass of water and her date shouted at her, that she was supposed to be submissive which meant he was to do all the ordering, all the everything, that was the agreement. He turned to the waiter and said, "Don't worry, you won't be hearing from her again."

After this exchange she made the quite baffling decision to go back to his. She had a rule that she never stays the night at these guys houses but he had a fridge full of some kind of alcohol that was expensive. I just looked at her confusedly, "Oh my god have you not heard of *whatever it was?*" Couldn't give less of a shite pal.

They started having sex and as it got nearer to him climaxing he told her to ask him who the girl was he was talking about earlier, the girl he lost his virginity to, the girl that that screwed him over.

"Ask me, ask me"
"Umm? Who was the love of your life?"
"It was my sister" and with that he came everywhere.

She then broke the seemingly forever silence by saying, "Do you want to see a video another guy just sent me? He keeps thrusting a butt plug in and out of his arse hole?" It was at this was the moment Lizzy came home, she was so chuffed to see the potential housemate still there as she thought it must've meant we were getting on well, not because she wouldn't bloody leave! Lizzy's face soon changed when this video was thrust in it, it was the whimpering sounds the guy was making that were the most traumatic, I've been sat here for a while thinking about how to describe these noises and have decided they sounded akin to Frank Spencer going over a load of speed bumps whilst in a Go kart.

We lived by Strangeways prison and on this same day a prisoner in protest of how they were being treated had been sitting on the roof for a couple of days, I could see him from my kitchen window which was the perfect selling point when people came to view the flat. Due to this traffic to ours was chaos so the same girl messaged the next day asking if she could try the journey again tomorrow so she can see how long it would normally take. "Sorry, it's been filled."

I started to gig with a girl called Merida, to be honest I wasn't that taken by her when I first met her as found her a bit cold which was odd because the girl I came to know seemed the opposite. She added me on Facebook after a gig and after this traumatic potential housemate encounter I put a post up saying I was looking for someone to rent Lizzy's room. She came to view the place, it was near two dear friends of hers lived so she could walk from theirs which was a wonderful coincidence.

She seemed a completely different person the second time meeting her, gave me an almighty hug, Lizzy was there too and we all got on so well, I wished we could all live together; although I think I got a bit excited and manic because Lizzy turned to her and said, "Don't worry, she's not always like this."

Merida moved in, I was so glad, we got on so well, it was like having a sister, I loved listening to her stories, she'd had such an interesting life. She was going out with this guy but said it was dead in the water so broke up with him, albeit eventually as she tried using weird goldfish analogies which he didn't understand so she thought she'd broken up with him but she definitely hadn't.

She told me what she said to which I said, "There's no way he'll have a clue what you meant, it sounds like you want to get a pet fish, you're going to have to try something a bit more traditional like, 'I don't think this is working any more?'"

Once he clicked, they broke up properly and she started to see other people, perhaps here did lie the problem. She'd settled down with a guy when she was too young and got a mortgage and all that then one day it hit her that it was too much too soon so left him and moved out which I think put her off the conventional way of doing things for quite some time.

We'd joke that her taste in men was "very dreggy" (dregs are what's left at the bottom of a barrel). I'm not sure if it subconsciously was something to do with her feeling she wasn't worth anyone better which is baffling as she was wonderful but of course us broken ones don't see that.

She started seeing a comedian called Mr Pickles who is best described as the comedian on the circuit that's the biggest leech. He'd make out he was a troubled working class genius but in reality he was an opportunist that thought about nothing and no-one but himself and actually lived in quite a nice house with his grandparents. I couldn't understand the want to be friends with him, let alone anything else: all he did was sponge booze, drugs and money off everyone.

I was living a sober hermit life at the time so his antics turned my head into a frenzy. He'd come around after being out at about 3am saying he wanted to see Merida but it was only ever a booty call / convenient place to stay for him because he didn't live in central Manchester but had work there the next day. He'd turn up and start thumping at the door like he was the police, it was so triggering. I'd end up answering the door,

"Keep it down for fucks sake, we've got lovely neighbours and the walls are thin."
"Oh hi Harriet, can you pay that taxi driver, I've got no money?"

I'd look outside to see a taxi driver waiting to get paid so I'd begrudgingly pay him because if I didn't no-one else would and I didn't want any more noise to be made. I'd then lock the door, go to my living room and he'd be there shouting,

"Where's the coke and booze at?"
"Good lord, I'll make you a cup of tea but that's your lot, I'm not sure what you think this is."

Whenever it'd become clear I was growing tired of him one of his grandparents would suddenly become iller, there was always something we were supposed to feel sorry for him about; Merida was blind to his shit. I was not.

Merida and I perhaps weren't the best match after all as she had just come out of a relationship so was sowing her wild oats which was totally fair enough but having these guys in our living space that I couldn't ignore was unbearable, even with earplugs in. Also they would drink heavily which was destructive for me to be around. I felt so bad for being bothered about it though because it was her flat too so she should be able to do what she wanted. If that wasn't bad enough I was now waking up in the morning, going to the toilet and standing in a pool of boy wee. The boys she was getting with were so dreggy they couldn't even aim their keg tap dicks in the direction of the toilet properly.

I told her I didn't choose to live with idiots like Mr Pickles and I was done with it. She said she understood, scaled back but then Mr Pickles emotionally manipulated so it happened again, I was livid and then it stopped. He moved on to rinsing some poor lad that had his own house and money his gran had left him when she died.

All was fine for a bit and then another lummox frequented. This one was a big sulky emo - If I'm ever in someones house and they have a housemate I'm always polite and chatty as you're in their home too but this guy was rude. He couldn't have given less of a shit about anything which maintained her interest in him for far longer than what was necessary. She was getting nothing, he'd just grumble, mope then drink all the pop and all the booze; he was a large grey cloud on giant oaf legs and she'd be eager to get the next date arranged.

I did a lovely gig that I do regularly, it's in a little village ran by an amateur dramatic society in a lovely little theatre. The trains back weren't very good and I knew sulky emo was staying so was glad to have some time away, plus to be fair to Merida due to my hermit-ness she never got the place to herself. I got hammered with everyone after the gig, I got dropped back to the hotel where I was staying, then wondered back in to town to find more people to drink with, drank whisky with some people that were quite possibly homeless, invited everyone to my hotel room then on the way there had the realisation it wasn't a good idea after all so sprinted off leaving them in a cloud of dust.

The hotel was in sight, there were a group of teenagers outside that shouted that I look like a man so I threw a log at them then entered the building and skedaddled up to my room which was very posh as none of the pictures were screwed to the walls. I moved them all around then needed a cigarette, someone told me once that if you smoke with a shower on in a hotel the condensation makes the smoke evaporate. I was drunk, got all muddled and instead chain-smoked in the bath which created quite the amount of smoke, and smell so before long there was a knock on the door. I answered it naked with a cigarette in my mouth and was faced with an angry but also startled hotel receptionist,

"This is a no smoking hotel"
"Well, I'm not fucking smoking am I?" I shouted whilst looking her dead in the eye and stubbing the cigarette out on my hand. She didn't know what to do or say so slowly started walking away but kept looking back confused, perhaps wondering if she was doing the right thing as I doubt any of this was in her training. I stood there, still naked, maintaining the gaze, believing I was totally in the right.

She was still there when I checked out in the morning which I felt was definitely adding to the trauma, whose shift is ever that long? Awkward fog clung in the air so I quickly vacated the premises to then have her chase me down the road which I assumed was a personal vendetta against me when actually I'd forgotten to pay.

Whenever Merida had someone round I'd be in total meltdown, I started to worry it was because I was jealous and madly in love with her but more likely was whether she liked it or not I'd put all my eggs in her basket as wasn't really trusting or speaking to anyone else. I was constantly holding a pity party for one which wasn't fair on her but also the people she had around were always such dicks with their dick-ness engulfing the whole flat; and I had no desire to live in a catacomb of dick!

57.) Final stab at the dick

I went on the online dating site, 'Plenty of Fish' for real this time. I found it comforting to have access to people to chat to so openly and freely from the comfort of my home and I hoped eventually to find someone to venture out with.

There were always a few people in my inbox I was chatting to. One guy (Skylar) I found his chat to be a bit dull but I spoke to a friend who said to go on a date with someone I wouldn't usually because how I have been doing things hasn't worked. I really took that onboard because how much can you really get to know someone just through messaging? I remember El Posho saying that she'd ghost someone straight away if they didn't spell something properly or punctuate right and that's not how anyone should be: don't let a comma stand in the way of true love.

I met up with him and even though he was wearing winkle pickers I knew the moment I met him he was a good egg, he instantly put me at ease, was honest, funny, endearing had an infectious laugh, got me and my sense of humour; it was all very easy.

We both had given up smoking but after a few drinks we both fancied a cigarette so off I went to buy some tobacco, he said he was worried I wouldn't come back, I was worried he would've escaped whilst I was gone.

He had four kids with his ex who he was with for ten years. He kept talking about her quite angrily which I thought was a red flag as he might not be over her but it turned out she'd put him through a lot and he was being open and honest, telling me all about it. We both 'put our cards on the table' for want of a better phrase; we were both done with games and nonsense so decided this was the way forward and if that didn't suit someone then that someone wasn't meant to be.

I kissed him and he sort of bird pecked me back which I thought was strange as felt what I was feeling was reciprocated too. It got late so I walked him to the bus stop like the gentleman I am, we were standing there for ages until eventually someone told us there wasn't actually another bus running. I told him he'd have to get a taxi to which he started waving his bus ticket around shouting, "But I've got this!"

We ended up having a lovely smooch, I told him I wanted to get naked with him but he looked like a rabbit in headlights and I'm so glad he didn't take me up on that as of course it was far nicer to build some sort of foundation first. Off we went our separate ways and I hoped to see him again very soon.

It's always typical of my schedule to be sparse one minute then rammed the next so I don't think we ended up seeing each other for a couple of weeks after that but we kept in touch. He wanted to see me do comedy and I was finding it difficult to get to a gig in Coventry so he said he'd give me a lift.

I'd only ever been in cars with experienced drivers, mainly comedians that become experienced quickly because of all the miles done in comedy. Skylar was a new and quite nervous driver who didn't have a clue where he was going and all of the above made me anxious. He didn't think to tell me he'd never left Manchester before and this would in fact be the furthest he'd ever travelled. If I'd known I'd have taken him somewhere better than Coventry.

He got on with the other comedians which is a big plus if someone can fit in with it all as it can be a strange environment and a lot of men get weird and feel like it in some way puts their alpha-ness into dispute and start trying to be the funniest which is embarrassing.

58.) Sent to Coventry

It was one of those gigs where no matter what the comedians did the people in the audience thought they were funnier. At one point an audience member said he'd been with his partner for 25 years and followed that with, "You get less for murder!" This got the best response of the night, the audience gave the guy a massive round of applause not having a clue that's one of the least original things to say, something we hear a lot.

The line-up was quite alternative which just didn't fit where we were so when we've all struggled because no-one's doing 'my mother-in-law jokes' the audience think we're rubbish at our jobs when it was in fact them being rubbish at theirs.

Every now and then I'll be at a gig and there'll be a group of men in the audience that are spread all over the shop with their wives hunched up next to them. The wives are made up to the nines but that's sadly where it ends, heaven forbid if their own opinion should leave their mouth and every time they go to laugh they turn to the husband first to see if he finds it funny as then it's ok to laugh. These fucking men are the worst.

At some gigs I'll be heading to the stage, they'll clock me then decide this is the best moment to go to the toilet or to get a drink, even if there's just been a break. I haven't done anything yet, why else would they be doing this other than the fact I'm a women? If they do decide to grace me with their presence they will refuse to look at me, often talking or on their phones. The longer I've been doing comedy the less patience I've got for such behaviour so will more often than not make a joke of how they're being (because that's my job) which they'll sometimes get nasty at as see it as a woman trying to humiliate them - Women should be laughing at their jokes, not the other way round.

"Andy, your jokes are awful, the only reason anyone ever laughs at them and never calls you out on your shit is because you're rich."

Sometimes even comedians you're working with's mask will slip. When I was relatively new I was playing somewhere considered to be the pinnacle of places to play, I did two late shows quite early on and at the second one the compere's introduced me as, "Here's a new girl giving it a bit of a go." It went *fine,* it wasn't good but it wasn't bad, they were mildly indifferent but that introduction definitely didn't help, I'd started on the back foot and afterwards he comes back on and says, "Ah that was a bit weird wasn't it?" No, it wasn't you crusty old bastard, I just wasn't a straight white guy blathering on about how shit his wife is.

I'd prefer it not to be the way but I find if the compere says I'm a bit quirky or something along those lines helps. A friend of mine says, "If you've got joy in your hearts you'll love this." Another time a compere said,

"You're in for a treat as there was only going to be one more act but another act has come over from another club and is going to come and do a short spot for you." Perfect! The audience are now excited about the act ahead so you've instantly got a fair chance, it makes no difference to the compere, these are new acts, no-one's going to be taking work off them, to give anything other than a nice introduction is them going out their way to be an absolute dick.

59.) Full circle

I was asked to compere the competition show I first saw Gavin host, to around 200 students: I was so nervous. I was asked to do it by the person in charge because they wanted new faces doing it but the problem is the person in charge is not at the night, the guy that does the tech writes the feedback then passes it on to her. The moment I got there he told me I was no good at it, I won't be doing it again, there's only four people that can do it, I hadn't even been onstage yet!

Once onstage the problem then became that I wasn't doing it quick enough.

"Oh goodness, so are we running behind schedule?"
"We're actually bang on schedule"
"It's not a problem then is it? I'm just doing it differently."

I humoured this guy for years when he'd tell me the feedback for me was one thing not realising the agent I was with was passing it on and it was completely different to what he was saying.

The guy that won the competition was too good to be doing it any more so I asked the tech and the floor manager if he could be put forward for one of the opening spots for the competition one day (unpaid, eight minutes is next step in progression).

I was told by both of them, "No because he was shit" which was wrong but when I tried to fight it I was told, "This is why you don't book it" they're never going to have the diverse range of acts they should because the club's got the sound guy and floor manager (who's actually an electrician) as judge and juror. It says it all too that the onstage lighting's shite, it's so bright it feels like you're in Shawshank Redemption, surely between the two of them they could figure that out as it's one of their jobs and the others trade.

60.) A guest in the lady pad

Once Lizzy departed from Beatrice's abode her relationship with Rusty fell apart. Bizarrely he ended up on our doorstep, he seemed broken, Merida and I felt sorry for him especially as his behaviour was that of a malnourished orphan. I once cooked a saag curry, there was loads left, I went out and when I came back he said,

"Can I have a little bit of your curry, I ate a little bit that Merida left off her plate and it was delicious"
"Sure thing Oliver Twist, it was there for everyone anyway."

Once I saw him wondering around with an empty bean can,

"Can I borrow this bean can?"
"Of course, but why?"
"I want to use it to wash my hair."

Who's using a bean can to wash their hair? Poor Rusty little orphan child.

Things with Beatrice and I had done a complete flip, we were getting on great again, I wouldn't really go out in the social group any more but me and her would go for nice country walks which were lovely and relaxing. Beatrice would say how Rusty cheated, emotionally manipulated her and rinsed her financially. I didn't know what to believe as when he arrived like I said he seemed broken and told a completely different version of events.

It turned out he did cheat, wouldn't admit to it; preferred to tell Beatrice when she brought it up that she was wrong and mad.

He was only supposed to stay with us for a couple of days as he supposedly couldn't afford anywhere else but here we now were months later and for someone that, "Couldn't afford anywhere else" and owed Beatrice so much money "that he didn't have" one can only imagine where he managed to pluck enough money to buy himself a brand new Playstation 4 with a variety of games.

Every morning I'd wake up to the sound of shrapnel due to the incessant war games he'd play. Our internet was awful at the best of times but with him now clogging it up 24/7 it became difficult for us who paid the bills to get online to get actual work stuff done.

The living room was now his bedroom, every morning after putting it off for long enough I'd have to go through it to get to the kitchen for a cuppa and breakfast and he'd start justifying to himself and I about how he wasn't going to do anything other than play computer games for the day because he didn't feel he was mentally up to doing much else.

Skylar and I were in the early stages of dating so it would've been nice to cuddle up on the sofa watching films but instead we had this bean can wally on it for months, he wouldn't do anything to help himself and seemed to think it was his god given right to be financially supported by everyone else.

I waited until Christmas for him to get back on his feet but Christmas came and went and nothing changed. Then he had flu so was on the sofa lurgy-ing it up for another age. Once it had passed I spoke to Merida about it, she agreed he should move on and off he went.

1:00am the next morning came and I heard a little tap on my door, it was Merida,

"Rusty's sleeping at the train station, can I tell him to come back?"
"Goodness, that's awful, of course you can"

I'm of the feeling now that was just to get us to taking him back - His dad lived just over a half hour car ride away for goodness sake.

Merida and Rusty were growing closer, I felt she became some sort of target for him, I had a feeling they'd get together but when I asked her she'd say she wouldn't get with him in a million years because,

"His nipples give me the creeps." He had very sad nipples.

I knew he was going to rinse her emotionally and financially: I brought it up with her, she brought it up with him and he said of course that wasn't the case but as if he would've said, "Darn it my plan's been foiled, and I would've gotten away with it if it wasn't for that pesky Harriet!"

This home was definitely the first place I'd felt safe in a long time so when these people were entering what I felt was my domain when I wasn't inviting them was another thing out of my control, uprooting what I was trying to ground.

It became clear Rusty wasn't going anywhere. It was obvious I didn't want that so it hung in the air like a big stench, I felt like a spare wheel in my own house. Then they were going out drinking then coming back at 6am and in their drunken states were leaving the door open so I was getting up in the morning, going to the toilet and seeing the door open which was sending me into an instant panic attack. I now longed for the days of standing in Mr Pickles piss - A breakdown was definitely brewing.

61.) A brush with stationary

Skylar and I were doing great: I was staying at his, was manic and definitely opening up that boozy wound again. I'd paused all gigs, was holed up at his drinking, smoking and having sex, all lots.

The days were dark, I was low, couldn't see a way out of this new depression I'd now found myself in. Skylar was lovely though, he was the only thing keeping me going but he had to work in the days.

He was worried so hid all the knives and locked all the windows (as he lived so high up) but whilst he was gone I improvised and wrapped my head in sellotape. I couldn't breath so slumped down on the bed, caught a glimpse of my plastic encased head in the mirror and started to laugh. Skylar came home, cuddled me, unwrapped my head, made me dinner and ran me a bath which was so lovely of him even though the bath was so hot it burned my legs and for a while looked like I had red wellington boots on. How he was with me then let me know he was the one for me, none of it bothered him, he never made me feel like an inconvenience.

He wasn't happy where he lived, I wasn't happy where I lived so we decided to look together, we fancied somewhere a bit more scenic as were both sick of concrete. I hoped Merida and I could be friends once I left but it was hard enough to make plans with her when she was residing in the next room, let alone when I was a 30 minute drive away.

Skylar and I moved to the countryside, Rusty officially moved in. In the years I left Merida got in touch once to meet and that was when she was gigging practically next door to my house so she was there anyway. If I didn't get in touch she most definitely wouldn't. I'd see how she was with other people and came to the realisation, "I'm not too sure what I've done but I don't think she's fussed about me."

Like I said, where I'd moved was 30 minutes away but she'd say it was ok for a lift if we were gigging together but then would always make an issue out of it on the day. I get it, I don't drive but you haven't been for that long and you know if it was the other way around I'd drop you home in an instant without any fuss. Instead she'd tell me to wake Skylar up to come and pick me up from somewhere more convenient for her at 3am in the morning.

Of course her and Rusty got together, they moved into a new place together and he rinsed her both emotionally and financially. He told her he had no money to pay bills but somehow found money for latest PS4 games. She started to cancel work because he'd say if she didn't come home he'd kill himself. It's hard enough getting people to understand mental illness without people using it to manipulate.

She broke up with him, he moved out and knowing she was away for two weeks left the heating on in their house and refused to pay for that and anything else he'd clocked up. It was a none furnished flat when they moved in so when he left he left her with all the furniture too which she'd have to get rid of as she planned on moving to London.

She was upset about it all and had no idea how she was going to get rid of said furniture. We were gigging together again so I suggested staying over after that gig and the next day I could put it all on Gumtree or Ebay to raise some funds. She enthusiastically agreed so I started a WhatsApp group of lovely gals as thought a few of us could help, we could get take-away and just be there for her as this plonker had knocked her off kilter.

The gig was in Wales, another comedian and I were meeting her there, during the journey down she messaged saying she was ill. This is going to sound harsh but she was always ill because of the amount of shite she eats, I'm not sure anyone could put away the amount of Pepsi she did and not feel like they're rotting from the inside out.

On the way back from gig she sat in the back ill, had obviously spoken to the other comedian about me not staying at hers any more as they suggested me going to his so she could explosively shit in peace then I'd go to hers the next day but he had a young kid and we both knew how flaky she was so she said to him, "Yeah just drop Harriet home" Oh like you do? When it was convenient for her it was fine. I was still supposed to go round the next day to help her with the furniture but didn't hear from her.

Finally we were going up to the Edinburgh Fringe Festival again, she said I could get a lift up which once again was a fucking ordeal, why did I never learn?

I ended up having to get an £80 taxi to hers, I didn't hear from her throughout the month but she did come to my one off Barking Tales night I did which was such a success that I was buzzing afterwards so asked her what she was doing, if she fancied a drink. She said she was going to The Pleasance Dome which is where a lot of performers drink, I really fancied going for a soft drink with friends so said, "Brilliant, wait a sec and I'll come with" to which she didn't wait, she just sort of wondered off without me.

Another comedian she was working with asked to meet up after their show one day, I agreed but they then said they needed to meet with a producer after but it would only take 20 mins so I agreed to wait, I waited an hour and then left. Neither of them got in touch with a courteous, "Sorry about that, it went on for longer than planned."

On the way back she made it clear that it was an annoyance to drop me home again. She was more than happy to have the free safe and well looked after carpark space (which are like gold dust in Edinburgh) from me for the month though wasn't she? She was talking about how she was going to get this PR guy for her solo show that made up this story for an act that got nominated for the main award a previous year. There was a crate on the floor, she was told to get on it with a microphone then photos were taken as if she had to perform on so it was a case of, "Oh my goodness she came from that to this, there wasn't even a stage, she had to perform in a derelict building, she really is the people's princess."

Merida claimed to despise *that* side of it the industry but was becoming that. Some would say it's not a bad thing to want more from your career and I totally agree but don't think it's necessary to manipulate or treat anyone like you wouldn't want to be treated.

I'd opened up about some things that had been happening at home on the way back and she was about as bothered as a very closed gate. We haven't seen each other since.

62.) The drive to drive

I drive now but oh my goodness, was an ordeal it was! I had to make myself stick with it, it was an embarrassment being such an independent person but still having to rely on people for lifts.

I'm the only person in my family to drive so it was never something I'd been around when I was younger. So many people have it programmed in their heads from the age of 17 to just get it done and I wish I had that because I believe the longer you leave it the more difficult it then is.

A friend of mine got me lessons when I was in my early twenties but it was horrible, the instructor spoke to me like shit, even shouted about how I put my seatbelt on before I'd even started driving. I gave up after the first lesson as thought, "Why am I going to put myself through some idiot speaking to me like shit every week? And he gets paid for that. Fuck off!"

Of course I'm in a job though where it is pretty much a necessity to drive. When I think about it now, the places I got to on public transport were absolute madness.

On the way to one gig I got so lost, disorientated, confused and ended up walking for miles on the Yorkshire Moors which was odd because when I arrived at the gig flustered and bewildered everyone was confused because it was a straight forward, none rural route past pubs and shops which I had no trouble at all with on the way back.

A lovely chap called Kenneth was hosting the gig, we always got on brilliantly and would go out for cigarettes in the breaks and have a good old gossip. On this occasion he was telling me how he was putting comedy on the back-burner to become a driving instructor, he said he'd like to teach me as figured, "If I could teach you I could teach anyone."

It ended up taking the poor bastard so long he got through six cars and went grey. He like a lot of people commented that I might have dyspraxia as for love nor money could I get my hands and brain to correlate. I couldn't contemplate how I'd ever be able to understand the gears, I had the co-ordination of an inside out jellyfish. Also I found that when I was moving the pedals I had to look at my feet, when ideally one needs to look ahead.

Once I was talking about this onstage, an audience member came up to me after and said, "My daughter's got dyspraxia" my response was,

"Oh goodness, I'm sorry, I haven't been diagnosed with it so don't want you to think I'm speaking out of turn or trivialising it in any way…"

"Can I stop you there, you've absolutely got it" he said and with that I stepped back, knocked over a speaker then thought I'd dropped a tissue on the floor (I'm always sneezing so keep one up my sleeve like an allergic magician) I picked it up and swiftly realised it was in fact not my tissue but someone's already used wet wipe so threw it away in horror but the destination of said horror throw happened to be in the man's face. The poor chap was trying to have a nice chat with me about his daughter and I've ended up lobbing someones crusty wet wipe in his face.

The theory test I passed first time which was surprising for all involved. I think because I could do it by myself and didn't have to factor in things that were out off my control. I just kept taking the online quiz over and over and over which really paid off.

Having said that I did cry in the middle of it at the thought of having to come back because there was so much clicking, I found it to be such a stifling environment. An autopilot reaction for me going in to any experience, especially one I'm not familiar with is to find humour in it, it's always been a coping mechanism of mine.

In slight defence of anyone that's disregarded ever helping me; that could've been a factor, "Well there's no reason to be concerned because she seems fine as she's making a joke out of it all."

They did not welcome humour in the place you go to do your theory test. First of all I got lost and ended up in a NHS building, then when I actually got to where I was supposed to be the receptionist looked at me like I'd just skinned her cat. She waggled her finger at a locker because I "obviously" had to put every single belonging of mine (even a belt and jewellery) in a locker and only then could I speak to this very sour faced lady upon reception.

I finally made my way to the room to do the test where a tiny man that looked like a snail sat at a little table said I could not got in with the tissue I had tucked in my sleeve,

"But I've always got a very runny nose"
"You might have the answers written on the tissue"
"I absolutely don't"
With that I whipped out my tissue to show him forgetting I'd spat an olive stone out in it that afternoon which went ricocheting across the room.

The practical tests were much worse, I'd never felt nerves like it, it was crippling. I think if you work in a job where that's the case it's essential you're understanding of that. The first examinator I had was so patronising that every time I did something wrong she'd tut and the more I did wrong the more she got annoyed which reflected in how she was speaking to me. I found her to be most unpleasant: I mean I was driving absolutely awfully but still.

I'd never had a lesson in the rain so when it rained on my test I panicked, didn't know what to do so was hitting what I thought roughly were windscreen wiper controls of which they were but seemed to be going ridiculously fast and quick, causing me to get in quite the flap and eventually the examinator roars,

"Just leave the windscreen wipers!"
"All right Tuttingkhamun, calm down"

I left them, "Thank you" she said, it was silent, which was then broken by the creaky sound of the rear windscreen wiper scraping to and fro.

Everything I was doing was worse than the last. My reverse bay parking went so bad my brain couldn't even comprehend how to do it anymore. I'd gotten confused by the car behind me having both his doors open in what was such a small space any - I couldn't figure out what I needed to do. My spacial awareness is none inexistent anyway plus just before I went in my driving instructor said, "If reverse bay parking make sure you don't go where there's a car behind" to which my response was, "As if anyone would do that" then in all the panic I went and did exactly that.

I needed to take a moment and Tuttingkhamun kept doing her trademark tut and saying, "In your own time Harriet, in your own time Harriet" and after the eighth time I snapped, "But it's not my own time is it, with you saying that over and over again?" and with that we stopped right in the middle of the manoeuvre, the test was aborted.

Another examinator was nice enough, I was fairly close to passing with him once but after the third time I failed with him Kenneth asked where I was going wrong and he said, "She's actually quite a good driver, she just needs to learn not to panic." Kenneth says to me, "So you need to not panic" Oh thank you oh wise one. You can't tell someone that's been panicking for 35 years to just not panic. Once I was on the dodgems with mum, I'd gotten confused, my steering wheel had somehow got stuck, and I was going around in circles backwards. Round and round and round, mum goes, "Don't panic." I panicked, shot forwards and killed a seagull. What was a seagull doing at the fair? They were understaffed.

I then had a suave chap called Tobias, he looked like he owned motorbikes because he did, always wore leather, must have been in his forties, had trendy bracelets, was tanned, held himself with an air of confidence and had quite good chat. I drove better than I had, did all my manoeuvres, had actually passed and then gone to park up, misjudged how much space I had so he had to do an emergency stop as I almost hit a car, in the last ten-seconds. "I'm so sorry, you'd passed but I have to fail you for that." I was so gutted and the guy whose car I almost hit was another instructor I'd become to know because of how long I'd been bloody learning so he was only there to see how I'd done, he wouldn't even of been there usually.

I had Tobias again and he wasn't as friendly and chatty this time but I kept chatting regardless. At one point I took a left turn too soon, ended up down a dead end so had to do a three-point turn out of it,

"You got an extra manoeuvre out of me there Tobias."
"I haven't because I told you exactly what to do."
"Right, ok."

My windows became so misted up; I couldn't remember how to de-mist them so was pretending they weren't that misty when I couldn't actually see out of my window which looking back was very dangerous.

My instructor was in the back and he was sneakily trying to crack the window but got told off for his troubles. The good thing was, I don't think it had come up before so he didn't know what to do about it so either put it down as a minor or not at all. I passed! I was over the moon, couldn't have been happier but when Tobias told me the news he was not happy and basically told me I shouldn't have passed (I think I only passed because he remembered the time before.) I didn't care though, I'd finally done it and couldn't have been happier, a whole new layer of life had been unlocked and as a result was going to be so much easier.

People were surprised I didn't give up but I wasn't going to put myself through all that for so long, put all that money in too but still come away with nothing. Plus, you know what they say, "Seventh time lucky!"

63.) Paving ones path out of a choice selection of pebbles

I absolutely love comedy, I believe it's what I was meant to do but has been tricky figuring out where I fit in to a scene that can sometimes be performing to drunk people that don't really want to listen to anything creative, especially at weekends where people would sometimes rather the comedian just called their friend a nobhead than did any material.

I've lucked out recently though and spend my weekends (when not in lockdown) as resident compere at ROFL Comedy Club Derby. I'm absolutely loving it as think I've found a way to incorporate my offbeat style with still the sort of authority needed for weekends, but my version of authority. I've been recording myself each night so could tweak bits of how I was doing things as I was going. It's a weekend gig with lovely vibes and obviously very funny comedians - I urge you all to come visit once we're allowed out of the house again.

Some comedians disagree with this but I strive to hopefully make change through comedy: I'm not trying to be Bob Geldof or anything but it is a public platform so I like to use that and try and make a little difference if I can. Reaching people with humour can be so effective, especially as any point made might not even be realised until thought about later as was hopefully all wrapped up in laughter at the time.

Discovering and coming to terms with my mental illness is all down to comedy, it's saved my life, given me a purpose and is the healthiest addiction I've ever had, it's helped me so I want to help back.

A lot of comedy I do and want to do has a mental health theme, I have an updated mental health show that I do at corporate events, colleges, uni's, drama schools etc to open up more of a mental health talking point wherever I am. I was on a panel at the Leicester Comedy Festival not long ago discussing this and I said, "I don't tend to do that material at weekend gigs to drunk people because it's so much more harrowing when something so personal gets nothing" but I've since done a u-turn on this way of thinking as realise it could be people in those rooms that connect with it most. It also sets me apart and invites a talking point about mental illness that perhaps wouldn't usually exist in such environments.

Above all it's what I want to be doing so no more pandering to idiots which is easily done in the industry - To play it safe.

Barking Tales became special for a lot of people. I had a year or so off at one point because I was in the middle of the sellotape head era but quickly realised that I needed it as much as the people that come do, perhaps more.

When I started I didn't have a budget to work with, did it all myself: charged £5 entry then with that I paid the headliner £80 and the opening act £40 and then anything left over I'd give to a local mental health charity. I became so anxious each month that I wouldn't make enough money to give to everyone and because mental illness is so unpredictable people would drop out last minute or wouldn't be able to work so couldn't afford it. I realised that's what it needed to be, even more inclusive so I scrapped the entrance fee, just did it as "donations after *if* you can afford it" and put anything made back in to the night. I can then see this going straight back to helping people that suffer with mental illness with my own eyes as oppose to giving to a company I've seen have questionable ways in which they do things, and with these things you never know how much of what you're giving is going in the pockets of the corporate people at the top.

This was integral in the change and success of the night as there was no pressure on me any more too, I now actually pay the headline act more because I save up the donations. I do it on a week day and the acts can try new stuff too.

The night's won two awards, the first being The Manchester Evening News / City Life Best Comedy Club in Manchester. It was so exciting, probably one of the best evenings of my life. I went with Sheila and Merida and we laughed so much and had such a great time. I'd bought a fancy new shirt especially but was so surprised to win that I ended up going to accept the award with my coat and scarf on. I hadn't a clue what to say, had a can of some fancy IPA in my hand and proceeded to tell everyone how it was making me very windy.

The girls encouraged me to have a photo with my award and post it online for everyone to see. I was so happy. We left the awards ceremony to go back to a pub, on the way there I accidentally dropped the award but luckily this one was fine. After a few more drinks I went to catch the last train home, Sheila and Merida stayed for a few more drinks, this was my first time drinking in a long time and I was lagging.

On the way to the train station a homeless chap asked if I had any change, I didn't apart from a limited edition 50p piece with Peter Rabbit on it so I gave him that and told him to get on Ebay as he'd probably get a bit more for it. *Really Harriet?*

I must've been everyones best friend on the train because the next day I'd been tagged by loads of people I didn't know on Facebook during the journey with each one holding my award.

The hangover the next day (well the next few days actually, but it was more the self loathing that came to visit after the first day) was horrific, very nearly outweighed the joy of it all to be honest and I'm pretty sure is actually the last time I drank with anyone other than Skylar on New Year's Eve (it'd be rude not to see the year in).

Barking Tales then won the Chortle Award for "Best themed comedy club in the Northwest" which I think we can all agree makes me well within my rights to start referring to it as, "the multi-award-winning Barking Tales."

64.) Swan Song

I had a missed call when I came off stage one night from a friend of mine in Cornwall I knew from the clubbing days, we always used to dance together and she's now Spangle's wife which is the most winning of all the combinations. We get on really well but never ring each other so for her to ring me, on a Saturday night too - I knew something was the matter.

Remember the friend that got her kid taken away because she left her with a group of swans? Lovely Soriah, the frozen chicken seducer?

I'd kept in touch with her as much as I could over the years but numbers for her would either change or not work and even though she had a flat she preferred to be on the streets so obviously wouldn't be on Facebook very often and had different accounts when she was. I'd check in but would rarely hear back.

Sadly her life revolved around drugs and shit men, she didn't belong in that life, had such a presence about her but she'd still tell you what she thought you wanted to hear and how she wanted things to be different but never completely made the change, the streets always swept her back in (which admittedly would sound more badass if talking about somewhere like New York, not Cornwall).

Last time we messaged she thanked me for back in the day. She was struggling, she needed a good friend. I never did anything other than let her know that's what I am if she'd let me, I told her if she got clean she could come and stay with me in Manchester for as long as she needed. I would've done anything for her, I really wish she'd asked.

My friend rang because Soriah had hanged herself from a tree on a housing estate in the middle of the afternoon.

It's heartbreaking, I think of her often, how she must've felt at that moment, how toxic Cornwall was for her too, she needed to leave. I hope this doesn't sound heartless, I thought such a lot of her but she was on a never ending rotating conveyor belt of that life that was never going to end well.

65.) Love heart emoji

My beloved and I fancied a break, I chose Malta as had seen photos of it online and it looked stunning so had wanted to visit for a while.

We arrived, the transfer guy was there to greet us, perhaps greet isn't quite the right word actually because he was not a happy chap. On the drive he had awful road rage then was trying to show me a video on his phone, I gave him a look as if to say, "Excuse me kind sir, I'd appreciate it if you refrained from using your telecommunication whilst driving." "Don't look at me like that, it's not illegal over here" was his response.

He proceeded to show me a video of his dog dragging six tyres along. I'd never seen a dog so muscly, even after Googling, "Very muscly dogs."

He told us our hotel was horrific. It was then I decided to look at the reviews (I know, what a tit) the first two reviews were "the food was like eating plastic bags" and, "We arrived to find a turd on the sofa in reception."

We just about arrived in one piece, checked in then I made the mistake of chatting to a couple in the lift on the way up to our room which meant later when we went for a drink that evening they came and sat with us. They asked what I did for a job, there are some occasions when I say I do comedy and as it's leaving my mouth I'm thinking, "Noooooooo, why am I telling them this?" This was definitely one of them. The guys face lit up and he was now telling me how he's never missed a Roy Chubby Brown concert in 20 years. "People think he's racist but he's just topical, offstage he doesn't think like that, he doesn't even swear, if you swore around him, he'd be the first to say, "Stop that."" Ah I see, that's totally fair enough, wouldn't want to offend the topical racist now would we?

From then on they kept accosting us with, "Listen to this really funny thing that happened to us today…" Followed by, "You'll have to put that in your show." Can't wait for my audiences to hear about when Trish's hat almost blew off.

We were the only people in the hotel under the age of 60, the majority of them were there for three months because they lived in a caravan park in Blackpool and there's some law or another where you're not allowed to live in a caravan for the whole year, only two-thirds of it, so they'd spend the rest of the year at this hotel. They were always carrying knitting equipment in one hand and a fly swat in the other as there were flies everywhere so they were prepared at all times to knit them little jumpers.

On the first morning we had to go for this chat with a man called Vince to book our transfer for on the way back. He asked if we'd like to go anywhere whilst there, everyone kept mentioning these bus and boat trips which take you to Gozo and then the Blue Lagoon. I'd planned to just explore around where we were as I do so much travelling usually so wanted to spend my holiday as stationary as possible and I'm not very good when my plans are just pulled out from underneath me without letting me know. Skylar's now signing us up for this fucking trip with Vince,

"Skylar, I categorically under no circumstances want to go on this trip"
"I just want us to have the best holiday we can"
...
"Eurgh fine, I'll go get my travel sickness tablets."

We got on this bus and I'm well chuffed, it's only us. Then we go and pick up every single moron in Malta and their gran, we go to about six different ports to try and get on this boat but the water's too choppy so we wait, the boat comes in, can't dock so goes back out each and every time.

As a result we're having to get an "emergency ferry" so everyone's getting off the coach thanking the bus driver. There's a strange guy in front of us that stinks of booze, is with his mum and wearing a suit, who wears a suit on holiday? He projectile vomits then starts whimpering. Skylar said, "You know in some countries where burping is a sign of gratitude, maybe that was the Malta equivalent of that?"

We were told, "Once you get off the ferry in Gozo you will see a lady with blond hair called Liliana." Liliana was from Blackburn. She ushered far too many of us on to a clapped out bus that took us to the strangest places, at one point we pulled up to a skip for 10 minutes.

We got to a little town called Victoria where we were kicked off the bus for 20 minutes to look around, we were told that under no uncertain terms were we to be late back.

We were back and waiting for an hour and 40 minutes for this idiot bus driver that apparently fell asleep. I was furious, Vom Jones had taken his suit jacket off and tied it around his waist, he was standing so close I could feel his hot sick breath on the back of my neck.

We got on another boat to the Blue Lagoon, this one was smaller and because the water was so choppy it was rocking so hard, Vom is now being sick in to a bin next to me, I snapped, "Everyone's feeling queasy, just got to the toilet you selfish whimpering bastard!"

After what seemed like hours we finally got to the Blue Lagoon but again because the water's so choppy they're finding it hard to mount the plank to the

Jetty so the plank's just slapping up and down so furiously against the water that anyone trying to walk across are falling off into the sea like lemmings.

Blue Lagoon looked nothing like the pictures, just more rocks, nothing more for as far as the eye could see. Although bizarrely everyone came back with pizza which I still don't understand.

Skylar wanted to go the opposite way to everyone else which I was most happy with because I'm not too fond of people at the best of times, let alone this plethora of muppets. We were chatting away, sharing a cigarette when suddenly he got on one knee and proposed. I couldn't believe what I was witnessing, I was totally baffled.

"I've been so nervous all day, did you not guess?"
"Absolutely not, I would've been less surprised if a peregrine falcon came out from underneath your hat."

He was a bit disappointed as thought I'd be more excited about it all, maybe even thankful so I projectile vomited and then let out a whimper.

Seriously though, of course I said yes, I was just taken aback because well, I definitely wasn't expecting it - There was nothing about that day that suggested, "Now is the time to propose" although the chaos was very on brand.

What was more special about him proposing though was that prior to this I'd convinced myself I didn't need medication any more, that it was stifling my mind so came off it and as a result I'd been an absolute dick to Skylar. I was always snapping and snarling at him, sometimes even screaming at the poor chap. He picked me up at the train station once after I'd been performing at a festival for most of the day and we had an awful argument, this might sound strange but sometimes I find we're just on different levels when I come back from something like that as I've got comedy festival head on and he's been caring all day (he's a carer, poor fucker never clocks off).

We've had this argument and I've tried to throw myself out of the moving car. The seat belt alarm is going, my door's open, poor old Skylar is trying to drive ON THE MOTORWAY whilst holding on to me, it was mayhem.

I decided it was probably best I went back on medication so had made a doctors appointment but couldn't be fitted in until after the holiday so my snapping snarling banshee-ness continued and he still proposed, still wanted to spend the rest of his life with me, I couldn't believe it, that really is commitment and true love right there isn't it?

A few years previous to this too (probably around sellotape era) I'd gone to Norway to do some gigs, definitely wasn't right, I drank so much I shat myself and was sick at the same time (I had to leave my trousers in Norway). When I came back Skylar greeted me at the airport with a massive framed picture to cheer me up of my beautiful mum and dad on their wedding day, I couldn't believe it, I burst out crying, it was so thoughtful.

When talking about getting married, Vegas came up as we both quite liked the idea of just fucking off to do it, I suggested getting a white suit, dressing up as Elvis for it and instead of saying, "I do" saying, "Thank you very much." He laughed and said that that sounded perfect.

Like I said he's got four children from a previous relationship and I'm not going to lie, that's been quite tough. At first what a shock to the system it was as for the last I don't know how long I'd been actively finding ways to work towards having an as peaceful life as possible then suddenly these very loud, unpredictable and to be honest at times quite feral beings came bursting in to my life. I waited at least six months before meeting them and would've waited longer had I not been sure about the relationship as that's what's right. At that time the boys were 8 and 9 and the girls were 13 and 14.

It was New Year's Eve and I turned up with pizza and board games, something they'd never played before. It was overwhelming as there was no structure, they'd all just shout and scream at each other, I considered coming back off the meds just to be on their level.

I came to learn how important it is to have reference points of good parenting, both Skylar and his ex had quite awful childhoods and because of that they had no examples to follow, whereas I could think of all the wonderful things my mum did with me and my brother and try my best to duplicate them.

We're lucky enough to now live in the countryside and strive for an as peaceful life as possible and that didn't appeal especially to the girls as they were of an age where they want to be out with their friends and I think thought our flat and lives were boring. The youngest girl and I didn't gel at first because I found her to be loud, confrontational, rude, with a constant attitude and no respect for anyones property. I needed to keep in mind - We are all just a product of our upbringings.

We didn't see the girls for quite sometime and then when I was at Edinburgh Fringe (remember I told Merida about some goings on at home)?

It was deemed no longer safe for the kids to live with their mother so were coming to live with us. Prior to this it was probably harder to build that bond because the visits had been more infrequent but all that fizzled away as these kids had seen and been put through far more than any kid should have to. They needed a safe, sober, homely and loving environment so that's what they got.

Their mother had such an awful childhood with abuse / neglect etc so I'll always have a certain amount of sympathy towards her but it got to the point where she was never putting her kids first - To help herself for the sake of the kids instead of putting all her shit on them. Skylar and I hoped the kids being taken away from her would be the shock she'd need to sort herself out.

At first she seemed more concerned about the money she got for the kids than the kids: in her opinion Skylar and the social had fucked her over, nothing to do with the fact she constantly picked volatile men over her kids and the social came around at 10:00am one morning to find her drunk with no food in the fridge / freezer / cupboards for the kids and empty bottles of vodka everywhere. We didn't realise how bad it had gotten, she'd apparently been warned lots but would always say, "Don't be stupid, no-one's going to take my kids away!"

We had a meeting with her, tried to explain that everyone wasn't against her, all anyone wants is what's best for the kids. It would be nice though for her to be happy too, she's got all this anger coursing through her veins which needs to be let go of, which I know is exhausting.

I was dreading that meeting, as were the kids and like my dads massive elbow I think I acquired a stress ailment as went deaf in one ear the day before. I thought the best solution to this would be to blast the deafness away with the power shower nozzle which funnily enough didn't help and my whole head filled up with water. It was unnerving to feel underwater and all times, I was worried my ear would pop in the night and I'd awake to us and the kids white water rafting. On our beds, we don't sleep in canoes.

She said she'd now got her drinking sorted and wasn't drinking vodka anymore, just beer and she was fine on that. The kids told her she wasn't and I said, "I cannot tell you how much I know about this, I've definitely been there, you'll just end up stretching out another alcoholic induced period which you think is a positive way to live before realising it doesn't matter what form it's in, alcohol is a problem."

We actually got on well, even hugged at the end of the meeting, she told us of these big changes she was going to make, we all felt so positive. Then the next time Skylar and the kids met her (an hour twice a week was agreed) she asked if Skylar and I wanted a threesome with her.

There really were no words.

When she was pulled up on her behaviour the next day, "It wasn't my fault, I was on coke."
Ah, ok, that makes sense and is completely acceptable. FOR THE LOVE OF GOD WOMAN PUT YOUR KIDS FIRST!

She got a job which was fantastic and was having alcohol tests so hoped that'd be another incentive for her to stop. Did you know they shave massive clumps off your hair for them? She'd say she was passing them but a social worker had already told us she wasn't, it was showing excessive drinking. Again she thought she could cheat the system.

The social worker asked what she could do to show her kids that they were loved and nurtured,

"I'd buy 'em an iPad."

She lost her job because she dropped a bag of weed in the staff room and has now decided all social workers can "fuck off," won't let them in and is now refusing to co-operate. Also after telling the kids she'd broken up with the latest boyfriend as he was sick of hearing about them / it was his violence that was the catalyst for them finally being taken out of her care she's now back with him which shows once again that she's put her and his wants over theirs. It's frustrating how she doesn't see this. I really hope she finds inner peace, owns her shit and then makes the change she needs to, no-one can do that other than her.

At one point she thought the answer to her happiness was a boob job but you and I know happiness will need to come from deeper inside than tits.

What used to seem boring to the kids is now a comfort. It's what we all need, routine, calmness, a 'normal.' I love these kids dearly, will do anything for them.

The oldest left school for a year with no grades so was hanging out with people she shouldn't for a year with no plans for the future. This was when we didn't see the girls all that much so I'd send her links to things for her to follow up but of course she didn't. It's put on kids when they're at school that if they don't do well in their GCSE's life is pretty much over so when she didn't she thought it was, she resided herself in doing nothing and her mother didn't look in to that as failed to see the importance as it was no different to her own path. Although she was offered quite a good part in a TV drama but had to turn it down in the end as she couldn't read her lines, surely that'd be a sufficient enough cautionary tale?

I emailed all the colleges in the area explaining the situation and one got back in touch almost straight away telling her to come in. Skylar said the mother said she was going to take her which I was chuffed about as it meant she was showing an interest. Then I was out one day when I got a phonemail from Skylar,

"You'll never guess what's happened"
"What?"
"So she took her to college"
"Yes?"

"And signed herself up too"

"What?"

"She signed herself up for the same course, dance and drama, they both start Monday"

"Well, I wasn't expecting that"

I thought about it and felt maybe it was a good thing, for structure, mixing with different people and a distraction away from alcohol but in the end she didn't make sure her daughter got there: so a combination of that, money not being put aside for bus fare and neither of them being in any way motivated got them both kicked out for poor attendance.

I then sorted an apprenticeship in beauty for the oldest girl (she loves beauty but says, "It isn't my passion, my passion is acting") but the first lockdown occurred and the apprenticeship became no more which was a shame. Then I sorted a place for college for this year to do acting, even though she'd got the place she was to get an audition monologue sent over which I thought was great because it from the off shows what's expected in the industry. I tried to help her with but she knew best, was at her nan's, assured me she'd send it over but didn't send it over. I even told her the deadline was a week too soon to allow for any lateness but she still didn't do it. At 18 now I told her to go in, she could still salvage the course but instead she got a boyfriend and focussed on him instead so the course was no longer available for her. I dread to think how she'd behave when something wasn't her passion.

I then wrote out exactly what to put to try and get a job but she'll act like I'm being unreasonable asking her to copy and paste, well to ask her to do anything. When I told her to copy and paste her CV into an online job site she didn't hear a peep for months which I thought was strange so investigated and found where it said for her to put her name she'd copied and pasted 'Hobbies and skills'.

The other girl has just started college which is great. She's also re-taking maths and english and has been told she should be in a higher group which is fantastic. We tried to find work for her too, she told me that when she does it herself she's offered loads of jobs but those turned out to be automatic acknowledgement emails, she hadn't read them properly. The boys go to good schools by us, I really hope it's not too late to get their reading and writing better. I love this family I've acquired, it's given me a new purpose, to help get them all on track. I'm not pretending to be their mum though, I'm just sort of holding fort until she sorts her self out.

In terms of wellbeing the countryside is really helping during lockdown, such beautiful nearby walks are good for the soul, there's even one with emus and peacocks. I'm doing bits and bobs online too, including catchups with the lovely regulars of mental health comedy night, Barking Tales. These are folk that feel isolated at the best of times, let alone when we're all on lockdown because of a pandemic. Strange times indeed.

Writing this book has been such a process, a chance to think and reflect on some things I'd so deeply buried. It's also a big realisation in how far I've come and how truly precious life is.

I'm so happy in my career and my personal life which has been essential in getting to the happy and fulfilling life I now have.

I'm definitely not life's oracle but I've overcome a lot, I'm genuinely happy, in fact I'd go as far as to say, "I'm loving life" (insert puking emoji) so have compiled a few things that help me live the best life I can.

1.) Listen to your gut

2.) Cut yourself some slack / don't be too hard on yourself

3.) Don't give yourself to people that don't have your back

4.) Treat people how you want to be treated

5.) Treat yourself how you want others to treat you

6.) Follow your dreams

7.) Work hard / as that famous saying goes, "Nothing worth having comes easy"

8.) No-one owes you anything

9.) Jealousy is an ugly trait, don't begrudge anyone else's success

10.) Focus on your own shit, don't compare yourself to others, we're all on our own path

11.) If you need help, get help

12.) Don't be a cunt

I'm at peace, have probably at no other time in my life been truly happy. I do a creative job I love, where I can be open and honest about my journey within mental health within that job - That's some sort of happiness inception right there.

Obviously as is the way with mental illness I still have low days, nothing is perfect, despite what we see on social media. I'm on medication (I won't be coming off it willy nillily this time) and that really helps - There's no shame whatsoever in being on meds, somewhere along the way it was put on us as a society to feel shame if you need a little bit of help for your brain but that's exactly what it is, you wouldn't have a big fat gaping cyst and not take anything for it.

I'm very self aware, obviously have known myself for quite some time so know triggers, know when to take it easy and when to take a moment to decompress and recuperate, not doing that at the time leads to a far longer ordeal down the line.

I've FINALLY got a good egg in my corner, someone that builds me up, never knocks me down: a wonderful, open, honest and loyal man with a big heart who if ever I'm having a difficult time will simply ask,

"What can I do to help?"

Printed in Great Britain
by Amazon